HOW TO WRITE A FIRST CLASS HOW-TO BOOK IN A FLASH

Bryan J. Westra

Indirect Knowledge Limited
MURRAY, KENTUCKY

Copyright © 2014 by Bryan J. Westra.

All rights reserved. No part of this publication may be reproduced, distributed or transmitted in any form or by any means, including photocopying, recording, or other electronic or mechanical methods, without the prior written permission of the publisher, except in the case of brief quotations embodied in critical reviews and certain other noncommercial uses permitted by copyright law. For permission requests, write to the publisher, addressed "Attention: Permissions Coordinator," at the address below.

Bryan Westra/ Indirect Knowledge Limited
2317 University Station
Murray, Kentucky/42071
www.indirectknowledge.com

Book Layout ©2014 indirectknowledge.com

Ordering Information:
Quantity sales. Special discounts are available on quantity purchases by corporations, associations, and others. For details, contact the "Special Sales Department" at the address above.

How to Write a First Class How-To Book in a Flash/ Bryan Westra.
—1st ed.
ISBN-10: 0990513238
ISBN-13: 978-0-9905132-3-0

TABLE OF CONTENTS

WRITING WELL AND WHAT THIS BOOK WILL TEACH YOU IN A FLASH i

WHAT YOU WILL LEARN IN THIS BOOK WILL HAVE YOU WRITING YOUR 'HOW-TO' BOOK IN A FLASH v

THE MANY, MANY, BENEFITS OF WRITING A FIRST-CLASS BOOK 1

    WHY YOU NEED TO UNDERSTAND THE BENEFITS OF WRITING A BOOK 5

    WHAT ARE SOME BENEFITS OF WRITING A BOOK 10

    HOW TO UTILIZE THE BENEFITS OF WRITING A BOOK DURING THE WRITING PROCESS TO HELP YOU WRITE YOUR BOOK IN A FLASH 17

    HOW ELSE THIS IS USEFUL 21

    RECAP 22

    ACTION STEPS 23

FAST RESEARCH METHODS 25
 WHY IS RESEARCH IMPORTANT 27
 WHAT YOU NEED TO KNOW NOW ABOUT MY RESEARCH METHOD TO MAKE IT YOUR OWN 29
 HOW TO DO RESEARCH SO IT DOESN'T FEEL LIKE YOU'RE DOING RESEARCH 42
 HOW TO ACTIVELY ADOPT MY RESEARCH METHODOLOGY AND MAKE IT YOUR OWN PERFECTED METHOD 44
 RECAP 50
 ACTION STEPS 51

TECHNOLOGY & USEFUL RESOURCES 55
 WHY IS THIS TECHNOLOGY VITAL TO YOUR ONE-DAY SELF-PUBLISHING EMPIRE 56
 WHAT SOFTWARE, TECHNOLOGY, AND DEVICES YOU WILL NEED TO WRITE A FIRST CLASS BOOK IN A SINGLE DAY—OR TO BE ON THE SAFE SIDE—A FLASH! 60

HOW DO I LEARN HOW TO USE THESE SOFTWARE PROGRAMS QUICKLY AND EASILY WITH AS FEW HEADACHES AS POSSIBLE 80

WHAT MIGHT BE SOME OTHER USES FOR THESE SOFTWARE APPLICATIONS AND DEVICES THAT YOU CAN USE TO CREATE OTHER PRODUCTS OR MAKE MONEY WITH .. 87

RECAP 89

ACTION STEPS 92

FINDING A SLANT TO PROFIT YOU AND YOUR READER 95

WHY IS IT IMPORTANT TO KNOW YOUR MARKET AND HOW TO DO MARKET RESEARCH TO PRODUCE A FIRST CLASS BOOK PEOPLE WANT TO READ 97

WHAT DO YOU NEED TO KNOW ABOUT MARKET RESEARCH AND FINDING AN ANGLE FOR YOUR BOOK THAT MAKES READERS WANT TO BUY IT 100

HOW TO FIND A SLANT FOR YOUR BOOK AND STEP INTO THE SHOES OF YOUR TARGET MARKET AND INDIRECT READERSHIP TO COVER ALL YOUR BASES 105

THINKING PAST THE SYSTEM TO CAPITALIZE ON TRENDS TO MEET MARKET DEMAND WITH PRECISION PERFECT TIMING 117

RECAP 118

ACTION STEPS 119

HOW TO WRITE HYPNOTIC CHAPTERS THAT BOTH FASCINATE AND INFORM YOUR NICHE AND MAKE THEM WANT TO READ MORE AND MORE 123

WHY IS HAVING THE RIGHT SYSTEM IN PLACE THE SUREFIRE WAY TO A SUCCESSFUL WRITING CAREER 125

WHAT YOU NEED TO KNOW ABOUT THIS SYSTEM BEFORE I SHARE IT WITH YOU 126

HOW TO UTILIZE THE BLUEPRINT TO ACHIEVE MASSIVE RESPECT FROM YOUR READERS AND HAVE THEM LOVING YOU 133

WHAT IF YOU REPURPOSE THIS BLUEPRINT 151

RECAP 153

ACTION STEPS 155

THE HOLISTIC ORGANIZATION PRINCIPLE TO HELP YOU SUCCEED 159

WHY DO YOU NEED A HOLISTIC ORGANIZATION SYSTEM TO BE ABLE TO WRITE A BOOK IN A FLASH 160

WHAT YOU NEED TO KNOW ABOUT ORGANIZATION AND TIME MANAGEMENT. 164

HOW TO GET ORGANIZED TO WRITE YOUR BOOK IN A WAY THAT WORKS FOR YOU 165

WHAT IF YOU ORGANIZE HOLISTICALLY AND FIND YOURSELF EXPERIENCING TERRIFIC RESULTS INSTANTANEOUSLY 167

RECAP 169

ACTION STEPS 170

HYPNOTIC DICTATION METHOD EXPOSED 173

WHY IS THE HYPNOTIC DICTATION METHOD A WINNER FOR MOST PEOPLE WHO WANT TO WRITE A BOOK IN A FLASH 174

WHAT IS THE HYPNOTIC DICTATION METHOD 176

HOW TO QUICKLY ACCOMPLISH WRITING YOUR BOOK USING THE HYPNOTIC DICTATION METHOD TO MAKE THE PROCESS SMOOTH AND SEEMLESS 178

WHAT IF YOU WANT TO MODIFY THE HYPNOTIC DICTATION METHOD 185

RECAP 189

ACTION STEPS 192

EDIT, EDIT, EDIT OR YOU'LL REGRET IT 195

WHY YOU NEED TO KNOW HOW TO EDIT AND WHY YOU NEED TO KNOW THE TIPS I AM GOING TO TEACH YOU 197

CASE STUDY: QUESTION THE EDITORS TO FIND CLOSURE ON YOUR BOOK SO YOU KNOW WHEN ENOUGH IS ENOUGH 199

WHAT TIPS YOU NEED TO KNOW TO EDIT YOUR BOOK TO FINAL COMPLETION 200

HOW TO PUT THESE TIPS TO USE AND KNOW WHEN YOUR BOOK IS FINALLY FINISHED 203

WHAT OTHER APPROACH MIGHT YOU TAKE IF TIME IS AN ISSUE FOR YOU 207

RECAP... 208

ACTION STEPS 210

HOW TO WRITE A PROPER CASE STUDY TO MAKE YOUR HOW-TO BOOK WELL-EXPRESSED.......... 213

WHY DO YOU NEED TO KNOW HOW TO WRITE CASE STUDIES... 214

WHAT YOU NEED TO KNOW TO WRITE A COMPELLING CASE STUDY THAT FASCINATES YOUR READERSHIP 216

HOW DO YOU WRITE A CASE STUDY THAT AFFECTS YOUR READER AND MAKES THEM WANT TO KEEP READING YOUR WORDS 219

RECAP 222

ACTION STEPS 223

LOOSE ENDS, ENCOURAGEMENT, AND FINALITY 225

WHY YOU NEED TO TAKE THE FINAL STEPS TO GETTING YOUR BOOK PUBLISHED AND LISTED ON AMAZON.COM 226

WHAT CAN YOU DO RIGHT NOW TO ENSURE YOU SUCCEED AND FINISH YOUR BOOK AND GET IT PUBLISHED AND LISTED ON AMAZON 230

FINALITY 231

BIBLIOGRAPHY 237

INDEX 239

Dedication to my dearest Jennifer A. Bonilla. I love you with all of my heart. You are my one true love!

Dedicated to the writers of the world who teach us, entertain us, and keep our spirits high—all by the words they write.

Dedicated to the number 13. I knew this day would come.

"Do, or do not. There is no try."

—MASTER YODA

FORWARD

WRITING WELL AND WHAT THIS BOOK WILL TEACH YOU IN A FLASH

A first class 'how-to' book that teaches others how to write a first class 'how-to' book in a flash. Finally!...Something refreshingly different—Something for everyone—Something that works!

—Syed Ali Shaw

Reading and writing are important in everybody's lives, whether they realize it or not. We all spend a good chunk of our waking life reading or writing, whether its signs on the road, restaurant menus, work memos, or for leisure. We are so fluent in English that we can spot a mistake a mile away, though some of the minor details may escape us, such as an Oxford comma. Without proper grammar, the entire sentence could fall apart and end in incoherent words that can't be put together.

Writing is all about conveying an idea. Without an idea or the motivation to write, there would be nothing to read, but it's not just having an idea that makes a good piece of literature. Making sure that the writing is concise and easily digestible to the main audience is extremely important. Any good writer should learn and understand when to expand upon an idea and when an idea should be compressed into something smaller that will take up less time and space in the piece. An example of when to compress an idea is if you're providing instructions on writing a recipe book. It's not necessary to insert "walk to the refrigerator to get ingredients" even though you could. You should expand on something such as what the words "beat the eggs until stiff peaks form," though. Not everyone knows what stiff peaks means, so expanding upon that idea will be beneficial to everyone. If there are inscribed instructions, good writing can cause a change in how well the person will understand and be able to follow them to completion.

When someone writes, they are putting down their knowledge, ideas, and/or emotions on paper for others to read, however, this doesn't mean that everything a person writes is a masterpiece from the get-go. Having an idea is the first step, and it doesn't even have to make sense to anyone but yourself. Many writers will put down a general guideline of their idea before even writing a complete sentence. Sometimes, incomplete and incoherent sentences can help to carry your idea further. Scribbling down a few words that wouldn't make sense in any other scenario are the beginning of forming much bigger and better ideas, and then you can expand upon the few scribbles until you feel that you're ready to write the first sentence.

The first sentence is usually the hardest, so a lot of writers will skip the entire beginning of some pieces. Skipping to the middle can get the ideas out of your mind while the idea is fresh, and it may help you when writing the conclusion and the intro by making sure that you've already got the events laid out. When you're writing, it's best to use your own methods, whether it makes sense to others or not. No one will see the process, but always make sure that you can put it all together coherently in the end.

This book teaches you all of this and so much more. This method described by Bryan Westra is incredibly insightful. It has been a real joy reading this book, and you can be sure you'll learn a lot, even if you already know so much. Westra's ability to teach others is one of his talents, and I can say openly and honestly that you will be astonished by everything he teaches you. I know I was.

Syed Ali Shah
Writer

INTRODUCTION

WHAT YOU WILL LEARN IN THIS BOOK WILL HAVE YOU WRITING YOUR 'HOW-TO' BOOK IN A FLASH

How would you like to check your bank account and there be more money in it than the last time you checked? You can! This book is going to teach you how.

You can take your passions and life experiences and turn them into a money tree that keeps the money falling into your bank account all year long—every year of your life. The best part is you can create this type of residual payment teaching something you love to everyone who buys your book. That could be a lot of people, or it could be a few, and you can decide what you want to do with the money you make every month.

Imagine a royalty check that pays your car payment. Imagine one that pays your house payment. Imagine one that pays both your car and house payment. It can happen, yet you have to create a means for it to happen.

Let me talk to you briefly about leverage. Leverage is what rich people love. Poor people don't usually know what it is. My father taught me about leverage when I was a kid, while playing with me on a playground in the park. We were seesawing back and forth. It was a lot of fun.

My father stopped after nearly catapulting me to outer space. I think he got too caught up in the fun and forgot I was a little boy.

So we got off, and stood next to the seesaw. My father said, "Bryan, you see this seesaw here?"

I said, "Yes."

He said, "Well, notice how the bar in exactly in the middle of the seat-bar. It acts as a wedge which allows one person to be up in the air, while the other person sits on the ground. But, what do you think would happen if this wedge was moved closer to the side you were sitting on?"

This was Greek to me, so I said, "I don't know dad, what would happen?"

Dad said, "If the wedge was closer to your end it would make it a lot easier for me to control the seesaw. This means, son, that it would give me the advantage and you the disadvantage."

I didn't really understand the concept of leverage then.

When I was older and I got my first job working at a fast food restaurant I was excited to death when I got my first paycheck. Finally, I had made my own money, and didn't have to rely on begging my father for money to buy the things I wanted. It was nice.

My father though asked me a life changing question the day I got that first paycheck: "What if you didn't have to work for that money?"

I was confused so I asked him, "What do you mean? If you want money you have to work for it; otherwise it's stealing, and I'm no thief!"

Dad smiled and came back with: "Yeah, but what if you didn't have steal it, and what if you didn't have to work for it, and what if it just was handed to you and nothing more or nothing less?"

I smiled back, and said, "I'd love not to have to work anymore at that restaurant and get bossed around by my bosses. But, how would I get the free money?"

Dad knew he had my attention and so he explained to me that I could create a product, let someone else sell that product, and keep most of the money. He explained it was a 'set it and forget it' process, where I only had to make a product once and then not have to worry about it ever again.

My dad was smart. I was unfortunately like a lot of people—I was dumb. I worked a good amount of my life for other people, then transitioned and got into sales, and finally gave in to complying with my father's suggestion.

I've always been a writer. I love to write. It could be writing down instructions on a napkin for a perfect stranger, or writing a novel, or writing the book that I'm writing now, and that you're reading. I just love to write.

So what is this book about?

This book is a book that's going to help you leverage your time for money. It's going to teach you how to write a 'first-class' how-to book in a flash. What's a flash? It's as quick as possible!

Of course, people write books for different reasons. We'll cover in chapter one some of those primary reasons. But, regardless of your reasons for wanting a book written, when it's written and listed on Amazon and other booksellers and it sells, you're going to make money. Money you don't have to continue working for. And, that's leverage.

The system I'm going to be teaching you in this book has been developed and refined through my trials and errors of having already written and published twelve 'first-class' books, and also through reading and attending numerous books and workshops by some of the best-selling authors of our generation. I've taken everything I've learned and systematized it into a near-perfect system that I believe is the 'best' system out there for writing a non-fiction how-to book.

My system takes into account all the things you've probably already learned through your investigation as well as probably much more. My system is big on 'value' and not writing smut just for the sake of selling something.

You want to write a book that is going to create so much value for your reader that they cannot help but give you rave reviews on Amazon.com and other sites. You want to make the reader so happy that they cannot contain their excitement and for this reason they 'have' to tell others about your book. That's where the 'first-class' part of this title comes into play.

I'll be teaching you how to deal with common unspoken problems many people trying to write a book encounter. These problems cause most people to give up. Even a problem like how do I write enough on one subject to cover an entire chapter will be explained to you—no worries.

You see I've meticulously done my homework for writing this book. After you finish reading this book you'll be able to write you book without all the problems most people encounter. Imagine, then, sitting down and cranking out your book, and having it up for sale online, and people virally spreading the word about how awesome the book it. Imagine though, this same book, was written in only a day or two—a week tops. Wouldn't that be something?

Well that's what I'm going to teach you how to do. In fact, I have included in this book my exact formula; namely, a blueprint I use to write every non-fiction how-to book I write (including this one). I going to actually show you screenshots and teach you 'exactly' how I wrote this book you're holding in your hands. I'm going to do for you what most people writing a book similar to this one won't, I'm going to be completely 'transparent' with you and teach you all of my secrets. It will astonish you, have no doubt.

Before we cross this threshold into 'How to Write a First Class How-To Book in a Flash' let me first ask something from you. I want to ask that you suspend your disbelief and doubt about what's possible when it comes to writing a book, and making free residual income (royalties) every month. I'm living proof that an ordinary not-so-special or well-known guy can make a living writing from the comfort of his own home. You can do the same, but you have to suspend your doubt, because you have to be able to wrap your mind around explicitly what I'll be suggesting to you in this book. If you do that, and listen to my instructions, you'll succeed in writing your book, I promise you!

Bryan James Westra
Author | Trainer | Publisher

CHAPTER 1

THE MANY, MANY, BENEFITS OF WRITING A FIRST-CLASS BOOK

When you, as a writer, are in alignment with your audience (reader) you stand a much better chance of connecting with them and helping them to get the most from your writing instruction. For this reason it is important to understand both what your reader hopes to gain from your book as well as what benefits you hope to gain.

When you identify both your reader's need(s) and determine how your content will help to answer and address those needs then you're being reader focused. Many new writers are caught up in this idea of sharing 'everything' they know in their book to let the reader know that they are the expert they claim to be. Let's face it, when we know a lot about something we're passionate about it is natural to want to share every detail with others about it. We do this in conversation all the time. When someone asks us about our profession or hobby we tend to smile brightly and begin sharing every little thing about our job or hobby that we find fascinating. The reality is not everybody is as interested as we are. For the reader, reading your book, it is more likely that they're simply picking up a copy of your book for the purpose of solving a need or problem that they have. They are hoping before they purchase your book that it will be their solution or answer. For this reason it is important to understand the differences between attributes, advantages, and benefits.

Attributes are the features your book contains. In other words, it's the content, how it's laid out, and what form it takes. The advantage is what the content does to logically solve your reader's problem. The benefits are 'how' the reader will feel after they walk away from reading your book and after having implemented you instructions (content).

Readers expect to be emotionally affected by the advantages of your content being applied to their lives. When you think of a problem I want you to think pain or discomfort. If you lose your wallet/purse and in it was the money to pay your mortgage/rent then you have a real legitimate problem. This is for most people going to cause them some pain and worry. If you write a book on how to make a thousand dollars fast, this would solve such a problem for the reader looking to make more money to pay their mortgage/rent, wouldn't it. Reading your book in this case would be advantageous in the sense that it would help the reader come up with a strategy for making a fast thousand dollars to solve their problem. The benefit, however, would be the reader not having to feel stressed out about not having the money to pay their mortgage/rent. The benefit is also the 'good' feeling that overcomes the reader when they have recouped their loss. I hope this explains enough about attributes, advantages, and benefits.

Writing your book solves a problem for you the writer as well. What is this problem you have? It could be several problems or just one, and they can vary writer to writer. For instance, let's suppose you are writing a book because your problem is you've just become interested in a new career in counseling. You've gotten your degree and licensing out of the way, even gotten some counseling clients who have successfully benefitted from your private counseling, but let's say you are wanting to get your name more out in the field. In this case, you've done everything you're quote unquote supposed to do to be successful in your field, but success can't come fast enough, and so your problem is not having enough notoriety in your field of expertise, i.e. counseling. You think, "Hmm…A book would be a great way to get some notoriety and help elevate me to expert status," so this seems like a great way to solve the problem you have. Make sense?

So writing a book is the problem-solving vehicle you've decided to take, the actual content you provide your reader make up the attributes (e.g., book cover image, instruction in the book, appendix, additional resources, etc.), getting expert status is the perceived advantage you have in terms of what writing this book will do for you (also called the 'function'), and how you perceive yourself feeling and being recognized for your contribution to the counseling field is the benefit. Other advantages may be more money you receive from royalties, and how this extra money makes you feel being able to spend it to buy things you want would be another benefit. Get the point? Good!

When you write from a problem/solution mindset you're addressing what attributes about your book will solve the logical problem, whose end result will be an advantage to the reader, so that a solution can come about. The solution being realized is the benefit and primary reason your reader has chosen to purchase your book. You're providing value from your expertise to help someone else solve a problem. In return you are rewarded in the form of a royalty check and positive feedback on the book seller's website (e.g., Amazon.com).

This chapter teaches you how you can align your needs with your reader's needs, by aligning what you want with what they want. If you want to be taken to be an expert then you need to align your content with the knowledge your reader needs. One way of looking at this is to think of it as a circle. You're solving your readers need and in return they're solving your need. No relationship can be one-sided and survive for long. You can't be a giver and never take; nor can you be a taker and never give.

Sure, you could write a crappy book with little or no value to your reader, causing them to waste their time and money on reading your book; however, when other potential readers see the comments posted on Amazon.com and other websites where your book has been reviewed, you'll lose those potential sales, because of the negative feedback received. There have been many times I haven't purchased a book I otherwise would have simply because of the poor reviews and feedback other readers gave regarding that book. This causes future readers not to know you, which in turn doesn't elevate you quite as high as you would have liked, and you lose money you could have earned had you written content that people wanted to read and would have benefitted from. Remember, this is not a one way street, but a two way street, and you must give to get and take in order to give more.

WHY YOU NEED TO UNDERSTAND THE BENEFITS OF WRITING A BOOK

It may be a reasonable argument to say that we start our lives with books; I mean, when we're little children our mothers and fathers read us books at bedtime. Out pops the children's book, and very quickly we find ourselves drifting off to sleep, dreaming happy dreams. It is special time in our lives, and the experiences are marked by objects brought into our realities. A particular book, one that your mother read to you, may be one having special intrinsic value; in so much, that you find yourself reading the same book a generation later, to your children. It had value to you, and you wish to share that valuable experience (magic moment) with your own children, thinking it will have the same special quality for them as it did for you.

Books have value that goes back to our beginnings (our roots). It's those magic pictures that we see, the ones we start to mentally become a part of, living the story as though we were the characters. The value that a book has is deeply rooted in our culture. We have an emotional connection to books. They represent times in our lives, which were special, which were most memorable, and magical even.

There are many reasons why people want to write books. It could be to connect unconsciously to an aspect of ourselves that can be felt and intuited; yet, perhaps, not so well understood when we try and rationalize it. And, sure, of course, there are many benefits to writing a book that are very practical. As an adult we likely formulate many benefits in our minds of the logical advantages without having to think too much about it.

There's also a deeper reason why people want to write a book. It is a personal reason. A reason not so easily understood. This reason is one that touches a part of the soul; that, creates a legacy for them. So why would you want to be a writer, an author? This is a question that deserves some contemplation. In this chapter, as I start to layout some of the practical benefits, ones you might have thought of already (or not), I want you to consider somewhere deep in the back of your mind that there are other reasons you're writing a book as well.

Why you need to understand these benefits is because this is going to set the stage for your book. This is going to be the foundation from which you'll start to consciously become aware of why people want to purchase your book, and help you focus on creating value for others. Building value is something many writers find challenging. When you're writing your first book it could be that you're not able to say enough about all you wish to relay to your reader. This is common for new writers. It is as though they have all these thoughts (knowledge) in their heads and they want to get it all out so that their message is delivered. It's as though we want to prove ourselves to our reader, letting them know we are the foremost expert on the topic we're writing about. We want our reader to respect us, gain a sense of who we are, and learn something from us that has incredible value for them. It's like the 'know-it-all' in our school days, who has to top us with their knowledge of something. It's not attractive. We actually shut those people out. Interestingly, we're all probably the 'know-it-all' at some point in our life. It's because we're so attached to what we know. It, in some sense, becomes our identity.

Some of the other benefits for considering 'value' rest in the notion that as we write we're learning ourselves what it is we know 'inside of us' but perhaps not 'outside of us'. We want to be able to consciously understand and state what we intuit inside of our mind.

Now I want to suggest as you begin writing your book that you put aside the idea you have to tell your reader 'everything' which you know about your topic. The reason for this is because were you to tell them everything you know, and everything you could learn in the process of doing research for your book, you would essentially write the 'never-ending' how-to book. You book might, in that type of scenario, become a doorstopper, instead of an eye-opener that is well read and well received by your target audience.

So the benefit for you should not come by clearing your mind of every nuance and detail of everything in your brain, screaming to get out to infect others, but it is knowing when enough is enough. Too much of a good thing is often quoted as being, "…a bad thing."

Why else you need to understand the benefits of writing your book now has to do with, in many instances, after a book is written, the author starts to have seconds thoughts; second-guessing him or herself about what was put in the book; namely, that which should have been supplanted, and what was left out which should have most definitely been exposed. This is because they begin to think about the 'benefits' after their book is done, and now wish they'd wrote it in such a way which could have exploited other benefits they'd not originally considered. Now it's too late.

For example, certain niches have their own lingo, which is used by those familiar and linked in to the niche. Sometimes people write a book without including a thorough explanation of the lingo, and often times exclude it altogether, and this can make the market shy away from the author, because their left with the impression the author doesn't really 'fit' into the niche. Had the author thought about this as being a potential benefit for him or her ahead of time, it could have saved them from putting out a book that doesn't get the recognition they sought for it.

Another reason is because you want to feel good about your book after it is finished; that is, something solid, something that possesses a lot of value, and also something that should you ever need to be a desk reference for you—teach yourself what you know. So I want you, for this reason, to put yourself into your readers shoes for a minute and really consider that this book is something you'd want written for you, were you them. Often times when someone writes a book they're writing a book about a subject they're no longer passionate about, but which they may know a great deal on. Like for instance, someone who studied martial arts for years, who has a vast knowledge of the field, but who no longer practices martial arts for whatever reason(s). When you write about something you're not very passionate about you need to pay particular attention to your audience, and put yourself directly in their shoes, getting inside their mind, and contemplating how they feel about your subject, and what it is they would like in a book and find to be of extremely high value.

The last point I want to make in terms of 'why' you need to understand the benefits of writing a book is so that you begin to get an idea of the practical benefits that will help you—the writer. This could be more recognition in your field; that is, instant expert-ship. But also for many other reasons as well, which I'll cover in a moment. These benefits may very well be the catalyst for being what inspires and motivates you to write your book.

WHAT ARE SOME BENEFITS OF WRITING A BOOK

There are numerous benefits of writing a book. Perhaps the benefit that comes to most people's mind straightaway is the idea of being perceived of as an expert in a particular field. Often times a person who has contributed a great deal to a field, or who has gained a lot of notoriety in a particular field will write a book to showcase their expertise. You don't have to be an expert, or well known in your field to write a book, however. Yet, after writing a book you may find yourself being perceived by your peers as more credible and legitimate—yes, even an expert.

The fact is what you need to know is that there are many, many, benefits to writing a book. There are different reasons why different people write books.

You may be wanting to boost sales for your business or your brand so that you can increase customer and sales opportunities that maybe you've not been able to capitalize on yet.

Perhaps you just want an extra stream of income. When you write a book you typically achieve income from the sales of your books in the form of ongoing royalties. These are residual payments that come in to you each and every month your book generates sales, and this can be for forever, way out into the future.

Many people write books so they can get invited to speak at special events. It is no mystery that writers happen to be some of the best speakers on television and radio programs. Because they've written a book they are elevated to the position of celebrity authority on the topic they've written about. The invitations can lead to more invitations, as well as be great marketing and brand building opportunities for the author to gain more dominance in their niche.

You can find many opportunities to sell your book, in fact, at different online and offline locations—for example, you may want to start a workshop, teaching what is in your book to those interested in learning more about your specialization. You can sell your book at the workshop as a back-of-the room upsell to help offset some of your event expenses, and also put more money in your pocket. This is a great way for people to also meet the author and get their book signed. People, when they know they can get their book signed, perceive the book to have more value. This is also a great way to advertise to their friends and family members when they showcase you book to their peers upon arriving back home from holiday. You can likewise adopt this same approach online through hosting live webinars and online trainings. The only difference would be that you'd offer your book at the end of your webinar with the understanding that you'd sign it for your participants.

Books also give you this elevated authority status. Many people, especially those in marketing, who market their own small businesses want to dominate their niche's marketplace to capitalize and make more sales and grow a longer list of potential customers. In order to do this, writing a book is one more rung on the ladder, so to speak, for them to achieve this celebrity-like authority status that makes them be perceived as the 'expert' in their niche. This earns them much more name recognition and influence over their marketplace.

Some people, believe it or not, just write a book for self-satisfaction. It is a task they've longed to do for a long time to the point where they no longer maybe know why they want to write a book—they just do!

Others write a book to gain respect. A lot of people wish to write a book; however, they never quite make the time for it, thus they never accomplish this goal of theirs. As a result they understand the process and how difficult and challenging it can be to write a book out to market, so as a result they tend to have a considerable respect for those that do.

Getting back to marketing for a moment: When you write a book and you get that book listed on Amazon.com and B&N, and other websites, it gives you a lot more exposure to your marketplace. It creates goodwill with your market and the potential buyers who would not only buy your book, yet perhaps also purchase other items from you as well. This type of exposure can come via Amazon Author Pages, and the Amazon affiliate program. This affiliate program is where other online marketers can join for free and promote your books for a share of the profit pie through Amazon directly. Not only does Amazon promote your book, these affiliates have a powerful influence over who else sees your book as well. This gets you more out into the lime-light rather quickly.

It could be you just want an excuse to market yourself more and writing a book can be an inexpensive, non-invasive, means by which to accomplish this. You may find yourself being called on to write blog posts for other online bloggers, or to write e-zine and magazine articles. This can help you get more name recognition in your industry, without costing you anything. Sometimes you may even get paid to write such articles and blog posts. This can give you a lot more respect in your marketplace, and get help to get more traffic to your sales pages, and website –and, even get others promoting you through social media marketing. All in all, this could be a fantastic add-in to your integrated marketing communications plan and holistic advertising strategy. You'll also in the process likely make a lot more friends and have people wanting you to associate and endorse their websites and viewpoints. If you play your cards right, you could find some neat ways of profiting as a result of simple association with others. Doing so will also widen your marketing funnel to cause you to create even more sales opportunities.

One way of going about getting some type of local exposure would be to start a meet up group; and you can do this by visiting www.meetup.com and either starting a local group in your area or else joining several relevant groups that have already started. Having written a book you'll have something to share out there with the group, and it elevates you in the group, personifying you as a leader. This could, depending on your locality, anthropomorphize you as a leader even, inside your local community, gaining you respect locally.

When you're done writing a book the sense of accomplishment can be enlivening. Writing a book actually forces you to step outside of your comfort-zone so that you can learn even more about your topic than you knew previously. It can for this reason be a very educational journey that takes you to some rich places mentally.

When you're having dinner with friends and family over the holidays a book can be a great introduction to tell newcomers to the party exactly who you are. It sort of defines you in some regard, labeling you as someone who is important and successful—accomplished! For this reason, a book, used in this way, can be used as a personal banding tool. They might not remember your name, but you can be sure they'll remember that you're an accomplished writer, and should it ever come up, your subject, they'll remember you and call you out as a reference. They'll likely be glad to have you as an important contact in their social and professional network.

Some people write a book, because inside them they feel so inclined towards a certain position or cause that they must write a book in order to get word out about the cause they strongly support. These could be religious causes, political causes, it could be environmental even. These types of writers wish to write a book simply to spread a message. It could be a message of propaganda or it could be a legitimate cause that warrants more publicity. In any case, this message they wish to expose to the sphere of influence holders in the circle they're trying to gain acceptance within. In this light, writing a book for this type of purpose could be one of persuading others to take a particular action or particular stance. This doesn't exclude, by any means, other forms persuasion either; that is, it could be that someone writes a book for the simple reason of persuading an audience to take an action and buy a product from them, or to join a group, or any number of other variable in which the writer wants their persuasions adopted or to help fill up their treasure chest.

The other facts of writing a book boil down to gaining credibility, name recognition, to get your material more accepted, and perhaps even gain you more resources you could call on as a result of having written your book and having gained some type of acknowledgement in your field of expertise.

A book can be a great way of condensing information that has been put out in other formats; namely, a weblog. There are many instances where someone has written a blog, posting thousands of informal blog posts, and over time they decide they want to condense the material, making it more useful to their already established audience, so the turn the content into a condense format—a book. What's nice about this type of scenario is that the audience and fan base has already been established, and so most will have no problem selling their book to people who already follow them, believe them, trust them, and value what they have to say.

A book can also get you higher speaking fees—for example, you can upon having gained some recognition from your book command higher fees when asked to give keynote speeches. The reason for this is because you already established goodwill and branding is now being associated with another brand. This type of co-branding can be useful for both parties achieving more recognition.

Speaking of fees, you can also charge higher consulting fees if you happen to do consulting. Perhaps you're in a business field, maybe one in high demand for consultants, trainers, and the such, and due to your name getting you there from your book you can charge a higher consulting and training fee simply because you're more in demand. This greater demand is a byproduct of your increase in intrinsic value.

There are the ancillary products that can come about from having written a book. In other words, you can repurpose material that's in your book to take the form of videos, audios, courses, and so on. This can create substantial profits for you beyond the monies earned from book sales. This can be a great way to gain some extra passive income through e-books, or podcasts even. To name a few others: some people will utilize content from their books for teleseminars, webinars, and again, going back to workshops, seminars, events, and even coaching programs can be developed around your primary product, which of course is your book.

Going back to marketing for a minute, you can use a lot of the exposure you gain from your book and the ancillary products to drive traffic back to your website and email opt-in pages to help build a list of potential future customers as well as track and measure consumer behavior from A/B split-testing ads to determine which ones are having the greatest impact for creating the most amount of sales. So in this case a book would be a great way to help generate more leads for your business. What's even more critical to point out is how your book can drive traffic back to your website in order that you're able to sell some of the secondary products you've created from its contents. These resulting products often sell for a premium over what your book sells for. So don't think that just because you write a book, and it sells, and you gain a tiny profit from the sales, that greater profit margins aren't reachable through having written your book.

We often hear of authors having a 'fan club' and though this particular book is directed to the non-fiction 'how-to' writer, you'd be interested to know that even 'how-to' writers can gain a following of loyal fans. This loyalty comes in quite handy when it comes to promoting and selling your book and products. People buy from those they trust and feel as though they already know and have a relationship with and like.

So you see you have a lot of different benefits you can look forward to after you get your book written. The sky really is the limit.

HOW TO UTILIZE THE BENEFITS OF WRITING A BOOK DURING THE WRITING PROCESS TO HELP YOU WRITE YOUR BOOK IN A FLASH

It's now time to take the benefits you want and use them to help motivate you and improve the writing process so you write faster while producing first-class content for your book. Many new authors can only think about writing their book, and that's it. They forget about their 'why' in regard to the benefits they hope to achieve from the finished masterpiece—their book. For this reason, I've included this chapter at the front of this book, first, so you might stop thinking about hurrying through getting the book written, and begin this book writing journey (quick as it will be anyway) by keeping your reader in mind always, while also the benefits you are going to gain as a result of finishing your book in a flash.

Regardless of what the benefits of writing your book happen to be for you personally, it's now time to take stock of the benefits and really understand what these benefits will mean for you. You see, people make buying decisions based on emotions and the relevant benefits to them. The benefits are the emotional associations someone has to the logical advantages. For example, someone may buy a car, but their buying more than just that; they're buying what that car is going to do for them beside simply get them from point A to point B. It could be the car they bought is a status symbol signifying all of their hard work and rise up the corporate ladder. This benefit is why they went out and bought the 300,000 dollar car, when the 20,000 dollar car would have accomplished the same goal of getting them from one place to another. In the same light it is important to take stock of what benefits you are going to gain after you get your book finished in a flash. Is it going to give you a sense of accomplishment? Is it going to make you appear more expert in your field or niche? Is it going to create a stream of income that will continue to come in month after month without you having to do anything else to make the money? There are a lot of reasons people write books, and asking yourself, after you take stock of the benefits, how accomplishing this goal is going to make you feel, is a powerful way to motivate yourself. You have to be motivated to write a book in a flash. You have to.

So how do we use the benefits to help us write the book faster? The answer is we start with observing what the benefits are. Then we associate the specific relevant benefits with the relevant topics in our book we're going to be covering—for example, let's say you want to write a book on how to be a better salesman. One of your benefits may be to elevate yourself to expert salesman status. Perhaps you've been in sales for a number of years and you've become quite successful and accomplished and even come up with an ingenious system for teaching other sales professionals how to sell better. What you can do is associate the relevant benefit, i.e. you wanting to be elevated to expert salesman, with a chapter titled, 'How to Be an Expert Salesman'.

By associating what you want with what other people want from you it makes it easier to write the chapter because you're accomplishing two things simultaneously for you reader's good and yours. By wanting to be an expert you must give your reader the expert advice in order to accomplish your goal. After all, and expert would know what makes them an expert sales professional and by delivering your unique spin on what it takes to be an expert, you prove you are an expert. Forget about the fact that just writing the book in the first place will likely elevate you to expert status regardless in some people minds.

The last step is to call attention to the benefits you want for yourself and your reader in your writing. For example you want your reader to make more sales by reading your book and in the process create more sales for yourself, so what you do is talk about how reading this book, in your book, is going to help your reader make more sales. You also talk about the fact that many people you've worked with have told you they wished you'd write a book exposing your secrets to salesmanship so they could do the same and make more sales. You simply mention these point in your chapters. Be subtle when you do and don't come across as arrogant or egotistical.

In my case I've written twelve books and my brother-in-law told me he wished I'd write a book on how to write a book, as he was wanting to write a book on some topic important to him. I thought about this and decided his idea was a good one, and I knew it would help a lot of people who get stuck in the book writing process. I knew they'd benefit by learning about the benefits and how applying the benefits to their own writing would help them write a better book and faster. The benefits are always why something is emotionally important to us. What's important is what we value. I knew I wanted my readers who read this book to walk-a-way feeling as though this book helped them to be able to write their book quickly, easily, and most important—painlessly.

HOW ELSE THIS IS USEFUL

I always think about the benefits of what I want to achieve from writing each book I write. Every book is different and yet the same. The benefits often overlap. For me personally it's more than just about making money. It's about providing value to others by imparting beneficial learnings to them that I believe will help them accomplish what they want and more quickly. Money is just the byproduct of the value you create for others. The more value you create, you can predict reasonably that the more money you will receive, generally speaking.

When you understand what people want it is easy to know what to write, as the answer is to write about the answer they're seeking in a way that solves their problem. Essentially, what you are accomplishing by knowing the benefits of what you want from having written you book is that you must connect with your reader and deliver on the promise to hand over the benefits they want to them. When you do this you connect holistically with your audience and self. You begin to feel good about the writing process and what you can do to help others get what they want. It's easy to write a book when you stop to think that what you're actually doing is telling people in your book how they can get the benefits they want from the information in your book.

Looking past this for a moment though it could be that you'll want to keep these benefits in mind when it comes to marketing your book later. The sales copy you write should reflect the benefits and by keeping what you want in alignment with what your reader wants it become a lot easier to connect with them in a sales letter. It's almost personal, I like to think; that is, it's like you are connected to your reader and as reliant on them as they are on you to help each other out. It becomes win-win in this type of scenario.

RECAP

At the heart of what you provide someone else is what other people will provide you with. Writing a first-class book requires you understand what other people value, want, and need. You need to, for this reason, ask questions to yourself that your reader is likely asking themselves. These questions might look like: "How do I solve this problem I'm having?" "How can I do this?" "What's the best way to do 'x'?" "Why am I not able to 'x'?"

We also discussed how to take the motivation in you when you think about gaining the benefits you hope to achieve from writing your book, and using that motivation to write excellent content that will be the benefit that motivates your reader to want to buy your book.

In marketing many times ad-copy writers will think about how best to phrase something, how they can make something sound more interesting, or how they can write something they perceive is brilliant; yet, the sales-letter may produce very few results for the marketing campaign. The reason is because the ad-copy writer has lost sight of his market, and what they want, and how they'll feel after receiving it. They also have used puffery, trickery, and persuasion influence techniques without really providing any upfront value to the reader who will be reading the sales letter. What the ad-copy writer should have realized is that their sales-letter itself could have and should have contained some value on the front end. In other words, it could have educated the reader about something which could have helped them, before they took the next step, which would have been buying the product being pitched about in the letter. In the same way, you want to write content that aligns proportionally to your reader's expectations. When you align congruently your content with your reader's needs in order to help them solve their problem, then the solution you give them to solve their problem is also the same solution that will get you what you want as well (e.g., authority status in your niche, more money, etc.). When you think of the solution to your problem also being the same solution to your reader's problem, you write more holistically, passionately, and carefully. In the end it's well worth it for them, i.e. your reader, as well as yourself, because everybody gets what they want and need and that's what we all want.

ACTION STEPS

Let me suggest that to the extent you do these exercises will be the extent to your success in completing this program. By 'program' I mean that you'll finish your book in a flash, and not sometime way out into the future, or possibly never.

You want to succeed don't you? By that, I mean you want to get this book written now and out to market as soon as possible so you gain the benefits you're desiring from writing this book. Let me answer that for you: The answer is and emphatic: "Yes! I want to get my book written in a flash so I can enjoy the benefits of having a first-class book published and making me money well into the future which readers will love me for writing and gain tons of value from!"

Good! Do these exercises real quick and let's 'hop' to it, shall we? After all, we've got a book to get done in a flash!

I. Make a list of the benefits you want to achieve from writing your book.

II. Make a list of the benefits your writer wants to achieve from writing your book.

III. Align quickly your benefits with your reader's benefits and use these as content in your book to help motivate and inspire your reader to take action on the first-class content you'll be writing for them, yet also to help motivate and inspire you to write the first-class content that will benefit both your reader and yourself. Keep in mind these exercises give you content to place inside your book as well as fuel for the journey.

CHAPTER 2

FAST RESEARCH METHODS

Believe it or not, some people really love doing research. Having attended a major research university while I was earning my undergraduate degree, I have to say that research was a never-ending headache that felt like an oppressive burden and even tormenting at times—that is, until, I cracked the code on some really amazing research tips that helped me to graduate Magna Cum Laude with a 3.79 grade point average there, and Summa Cum Laude with a 4.00 grade point average when I earned my MBA in Marketing from another elite private university. In this chapter I'm going to teach you my refined research techniques to make it possible for you to model the same success and get your first-class book finished pronto—I mean seriously in a flash! Strap on your seat-belt, because this is going to be an exciting and even 'fun' ride, I promise you.

In chapter 3, here, I'm going to hint at some of the different resources I'll be covering in greater detail with you later in this book. This doesn't mean I want you getting caught up in all the details of this technology and software right now. I would prefer rather that you keep your focus entirely on what this chapter is about—namely research.

There is an approach I'll be sharing with you in this chapter that will have you doing research in a way that is fun and enjoyable, while also keeping your attention and letting you utilize the best parts of yourself in writing your book. I'm also going to teach you some of the different techniques you can employ to make your research much, much, faster. The less time you spend having to research, the more time you can spend writing your book and getting it finished. You can't write a book if you have nothing to say, and for this reason research is vital. You might think of research as the ugly sister of writing. The two are conjoined twins who are inseparable from one another.

In order to fashion your book in a way that your readers will appreciate and learn from you must know and have learned what it is you'll be teaching in your 'how-to' book. That's what the nature of this research methodology, which I'll be teaching you, is all about. The last thing I'll talk on in this chapter will be some logical rational as to why you may want to write a book in a flash. I'll talk about keeping focus, and why writing a book in a very short period of time increases your probability that your book will be of a higher quality and value to your readership, and I'll give you some food for thought, while allowing you some opportunity to explore through application what approach to writing will work best for you given the nature of your personality and aptitude to take action on completing works tasks. I realize in writing this book that no reader is exactly the same, things the same way, or learns in the same way. For this reason I've designed this book to give you some latitude to explore for yourself possible alternatives that may work best for the whole of who you are. These very possibly may vary vastly away from the method I share in this book. The reason being is I want you to find the method of writing that works best for you. This isn't about me—rather, it's all about you. You are the reader and for this reason I want you do get the most value from this book as possible, and I do not want to trap you in a box of logic and reason that would take that away from you. So I hope you enjoy this journey, and most importantly—make it your own journey!

WHY IS RESEARCH IMPORTANT

Sometimes you have to standup and standout to get noticed; to gain the recognition you know you deserve. It is important when you're writing a book to keep your reader's attention throughout. If you go back and recall some of the books you might have read in the past you'll probably start to recognize certain patterns emerge. These patterns are associated with the good books you remember well, and the not so good books that you wish you could forget.

In order to really write a compelling book people take seriously and can believe in and even wish they'd come up with the content themselves; namely, because they value it as brilliant, you have to get your research right first, in order to draw your own conclusions, share your findings, and make sense of the never-ending flow of data out there to be able to share it with your reader. Most readers wouldn't spend 10 minutes sifting through all this chaos. You may feel like them also; feeling about this the same way, that is.

The good news is you're not the only one who dreads the laborious task of data mining. Why you ask? The answer is because if you dread sifting through all this data, chances are good that your competition does too. This means giving you an advantage, providing you take a few minutes to learn the secret to doing really good research.

People always have preferences in who they want to know, trust, and like (love?). Doing great research and presenting it in a very digestible format is the critical 'key' to ensuring your readers perceive you as the expert and not the next guy or gal.

When you know of a good system for doing research that works and lets you accomplish all this required research fast and easy then it's vital that you become in the habit of doing regular research for your writing projects. If you have old belief patterns about how painstaking researching has to be, keep in mind that the world is a changing place, and with the technology we have today research can be done in a fraction of the time and done employing more enjoyable methods.

I'm going to be teaching you some of my secrets to doing fast accurate research throughout this chapter. My advice is for you to cultivate a positive attitude whereas researching is concerned.

What's nice about doing research is you're always learning and improving your own self, which makes you more valuable to your marketplace. All the experts I've ever run into and had a quick chat with all commented that learning and researching were embedded in their psyche. They formed positive habits early in life that have carried them to wonderful places throughout.

Imagine being able to frequently learn something new and then be able to take that knowledge and earn income from it. I mean after all that is why college students go to college and learn how to do new things—I'm talking about so they can get a job after graduating. However, even once they get themselves a job, they still must master learning new skills, and this is something that never ends. Learning is a never ending process –and, so, you might as well make some money from what you learn. Even if it isn't through the outlet of a job.

WHAT YOU NEED TO KNOW NOW ABOUT MY RESEARCH METHOD TO MAKE IT YOUR OWN

The first thing I want to do is walk you through the overall process though how I do research. The first you need to understand it that you are taking a broad topic, which is what your book is supposedly about. Then you're making sense of the broad topic by chunking down into smaller more manageable parts. You structure you book by vivisecting your book idea down into chapters, and then subtopics, and in cases it may even be necessary and appropriate to chunk down even smaller into subsections of a subtopic.

Once you have your chapters and have those broken down into subtopics and subsections you're ready to start doing research. You'll be combining writing and research as you work on your book. This way you don't feel trapped for hours doing research or trapped for hours writing page after page. It sort of breaks up the monotony, and gives your brain a rest from doing the same tedious activity for too long a period. So do research then write on that research, do research then write on that research, and continue alternating between researching and writing as you work through completing your book.

I will be teaching you in a future chapter in this book exactly how I structure chapters, subtopics, and subsections, so for now just focus on learning how to do quick, yet highly effective research. You'll be able to apply this later on when we get into the writing aspects. I just want you to have it in your head how to do research, as all of this will make far greater sense as you continue progressing through this book.

I'll be teaching you about Evernote.com and how I leverage it to write my books later-on. Just know for now that it is a free note compiling application that lets you do several things amazingly well: (a) lets you take notes on the go with your Android or Apple smartphone, (b) lets you dictate into your phone and sync those audio notes directly onto other devices (e.g., laptop), (c) lets you take photos with your smartphone to sync those pictures directly onto other devices (e.g., laptop), (d) lets you clip screenshots and store them as notes, and (e) it lets you organize everything nice and easily while giving you short summaries of which note contains what information.

Again, I'll be covering this in more detail later, so keep you focus on just doing research for right now. Stay with me, this part is critically important, if you want to get this book done in a flash.

Now I want to talk to you about two types of research you can do. You can do offline research; however, you can also do online research—these are the two types of research.

Now for a lot of people who want to write a book on a particular topic they in most cases already have a small or in some cases a huge personal library from which to research from. If this is the case, and you know where to find the information you're writing about quickly, then this will most likely be the fastest way to get your research compiled. For offline interviews I like to do expert interviews. By expert, I simply mean someone involved in the industry I'm writing on, passionate about the subject matter, and who doesn't seem to mind giving me 5, 10, 15, or 20 minutes of their time.

You can utilize a telephone conferencing platform that allows you to record the interview, where both of you are on the conference line at the same time. Many of these are free to so setup. My favorite is: www.freeconferencecall.com. What's nice about it is it allows you to have a free webpage with the call-in details to send out instantly to your email list. You can also record the calls, have up to 1000 people on the line, and download the recordings as MP3 files to repurpose later as future products or marketing communication messages.

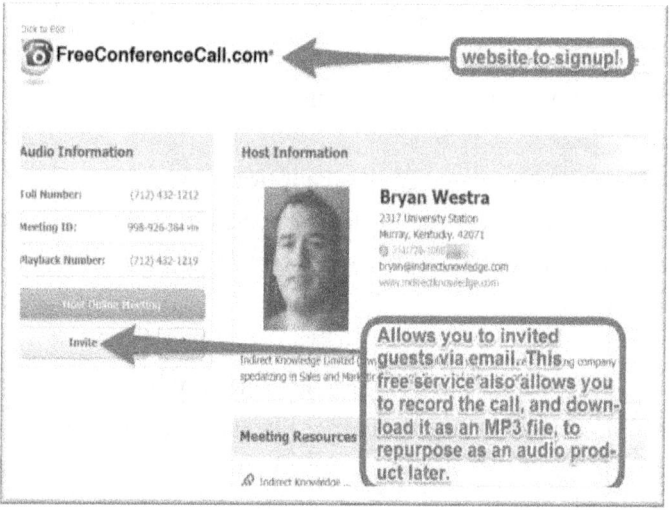

There are of course other platforms you can utilize that may be more comfortable or useful for you. By all means find what works for you and use that.

Skype is another option for recording both audio and video. What you'll need to do is purchase a Skype plugin that will integrate with your Skype platform, in order to record your calls and videos. I personally tend to take this approach over having someone dial into a conference call, if I'm simply communicating with one person for the purpose of doing a quick interview.

My personal preference, and I'll tell you honestly that I've tried several different Skype recording plugins, but I prefer the quality of Super TinTin (www.supertintin.com)

What Super TinTin does is allow you to record both sides of the conversation, and even record both sides of the video; that is to say, both sides of the video (i.e., your screen and theirs). Keep in mind, however, that it is illegal to record people without telling them they are being recorded in many locals. So always, always, always, tell the person you are recording them. What's nice about using Super TinTin is that you can actually repurpose the videos and audios your produce and resell them as standalone products, or offer them as incentive for someone to join your email list.

Another interview solution is to ask some question on Facebook or some other social media site, and provoke people to answer the questions. This is a great way to get research and feedback from others.

Another offline research resource are libraries. Libraries are important as it helps underprivileged people have an opportunity to learn what others learn in expensive colleges, without having to incur the costs. You can learn information free of charge and apply it into your book. The nice thing about most libraries are that they're staffed with knowledgeable people who love to do research and help other people with their research. If you ask a reference librarian a question you can be assured that you'll be pointed in the right direct, if not taken by the hand to exactly what it is you're looking for. Most libraries these days also have internet, and assuming you have a smartphone with the Evernote app downloaded you'll be able to quickly take pictures of book pages and sync them into your Evernote account for when you're ready to start compiling and organizing your research.

Offline, you can also call on special interest groups. This could be a local meetup.com group, that you've either started, or one that is already meeting up regularly, and you can pay them a visit, unless of course you're already a regular member. And, feel welcome to go and get some feedback, but also a great resource for finding people to interview as well. Often there are experts in a particular field that attend these types of groups regularly. You can rub elbows and add people to your own professional network, and get the much needed material for your book that you need. Some of my best ideas have come from attending these type of group get-togethers.

Another way to do offline research is through attending training courses. You can purchase programs that have been of live events from the past to watch and learn from in the comfort of your own home. These can be related to whatever it is you're trying to teach other people how to do in your own book. Because, surely other people have written and trained on what your interest is as well, and you may need only search them out and…hey…possibly learn something new yourself!!! Just finding those resources is really what it's all about. Even better though, you could register and attend live events if time and money permit. These can be workshops others in your field put on. They can be great to learn new things and practice your skillset. They can also be great places for interviewing and picking the brains of your market as well as the other experts operating in your niche.

The online resources are the ones I tend to utilize most. This isn't to say I don't utilize offline resources for almost every single book I write, because I do, but it is to say that the research can be handled quickly and efficiently making the book 100x faster to put together and write. You can also do fast academic research online through sites like Google Scholar (http://scholar.google.com). These are scholarly resources compiled by Google that are searchable through keywords you enter into a Google Search box.

Most of the time this scholarly information is free to access; however, there are some instances where you'll be routed to another website where it will require you to sign up to access the information, and get like a free trial. And, some that will require a purchased subscription in order to access the information. Most of the time it's not necessary to make a purchase, however. This is a great scholarly research avenue if you happen to be on a budget and every penny matters. Google Scholar is a great place to find PDF documents of scholarly journal articles, and it saves you a tremendous amount of time in finding accurate and relevant information that is accepted by the academic community as being legitimate.

There is also general knowledge you can find through weblogs, YouTube videos, Wikipedia, websites, and online forums that are specifically focused on your topic and what you need to research.

Now, sidestepping just for a moment, I want to share one of my great research secrets. YouTube has many relevant videos that you can pick up and summarize in a couple minutes quickly; rather, than having to read a ton of webpages and other print resources. Many of these videos are surprisingly put together well, and you can tell the author of many of these well put together videos put in a lot of time getting them perfected. Much of the content you will find on some of these well put together videos the authors list the references they used to pull the data at the end of the videos or in the comments section below the video. Why this is a powerful way to do research quickly is because someone else has already done the research for you—all you need to do is watch the video and summarize it into your book and make it yours. Watching something like a video can be a much more entertaining way of doing research. For longer videos you can set them to play, and be listening to them, as you fix a mid-afternoon snack for yourself, or do some other type of activity (e.g., yoga on the floor of your home office). Just don't mention to other serious yogis that you're 'killing' two birds with one stone, as they might take you literal and stone you.

The second major research secret I'll share with you is how I use Wikipedia.com. In the academic community Wikipedia is shunned in terms of being a place to do research. If you're in college pursuing a degree you'll probably get deducted points and warned if you include a Wikipedia reference in a paper you submit for a grade. Here's the secret though: Most Wikipedia pages are cited from academic and more legitimate sources. The citations are most always included as well at the bottom of the Wikipedia posting. Often times these citations have hyperlinks back linking to the original high quality source. So what you do is Wikipedia what you need, survey it to learn and extract what you need, and then back track to the original source and quickly skim the sections relevant to your research and include that in your book (in your own words of course). Why this is a shortcut is because all the resources you may need may be listed right there on Wikipedia, and the citations are already done for you. You need only copy and paste the citation into your bibliography. In this way too you can digest from the Wiki page what might require you reading several 300 – 500 page books to discover on your own. This is a definite time saver and I've always felt like I've learned a lot more in the general sense by surveying the Wikipedia page.

You can also do online interviews and research by visiting online forums. You can ask a question on a forum and often times get many different responses that can be used in your book in some capacity. Of course you can pick the best answer or a combination of answers and utilize what's best for you. This can take some time however – and, for the purposes of writing a book in a flash may not be a viable way to do research. However, if you have a book that you don't mind putting some research time into this may be a great way to come up with some powerful content for your book.

Perhaps your best references for the purpose of writing a book in a flash are going to be Google Scholar, YouTube videos, and Wikipedia references that you cross reference for your book.

So this is the wrap up of how I do research for books. It is very quick and very fast. It is also entertaining. If you've ever wanted to learn how to do something—for example, fix the starter on your 1989 Jeep Cherokee YouTube is a great site to find a video to do just that. So you'd be surprised what you can figure out. Another example might be that you're writing a book on Excel (I had to learn Excel for college), then let me assure you there are TONS of videos on learning Excel. There's no need for you to spend a lot of money to go to a workshop to learn it, when there's every tutorial imaginable right there in front of you on YouTube. YouTube is great because you utilize different representational systems while you learn to help you learn things quicker (e.g., auditory, and visual). I used to joke with people that I could have learnt everything I did in college from simply (and for free) watching YouTube videos. Probably the truth!

So let's talk now about what you're going to specifically be researching. The things you want to look for are relevant case studies. By relevant I mean timely. These are cases that are the most recent studies that you may even have heard about recently in the media. You also want to look for compelling stories. If something catches your eye; taking you off guard, then chances are it will take other people off guard as well. Stories are captivatingly hypnotic and a perfect tool for keeping your audience's attention. So one thing you might want to do is insert some of these compelling stories to your book to make it richer and interesting to your readership. People love stories.

You can also get research to support the arguments you want to make. Though facts alone can be boring for most people, without facts you lose a lot of credibility with your reader. The key is to find relevant facts and research from scholarly articles and case studies and make them almost conversational in your own book; as if, you are sharing something interesting with a friend you happen to be talking to while enjoying a lunch date together. The last think I want to say about this is how the people who have done the research in the past that you're recounting to someone else are your backers; that is, these people are people in your corner who are on your side, and the more people on your side, the more likely someone reading your book is to trust you and believe what you tell them is true. It's sort of like I could tell you something, but it's far more believable if I tell you that twenty other people said the same thing was true. You'd more likely trust the group over the individual telling you something. Keep this in mind when you are writing your own book.

Another way to research is to buy the top three books written about your topic and read over the table of contents of each of these books and then skim the main points to get an idea of what the 'best of the best' in your field are saying and learn how they're communicating these ideas in their own book. So you can visit Amazon.com and pickup these books instantly on Kindle, and already have three powerful table of contents that you can use to structure your own book after. You don't have to necessarily imagine what each of your own chapters are going to be about, as you can use the top experts' tables of contents and figure out how you might want to organize your own chapters. This save a massive amount of time when you're wondering what your chapters should be about. Look for patterns of repetition in all three of these books and know that you'll likely want to include all of those repeating chapters in your own book. Then you can most certainly, and I would of course expect you to, have a couple of chapters that are cutting-edge and powerfully unrelated, but a contribution to the field. This is where your own creativity can come in useful. Modeling the success of others is a great to become successful yourself. By being original and differentiating yourself from your competition by offering more even more value than they are offering is a great way to dominate your niche.

I know all of this information is a lot to perhaps take in, so I've taken the liberty of mind mapping the various research avenues to serve as a cheat sheet/memory jogger for you.

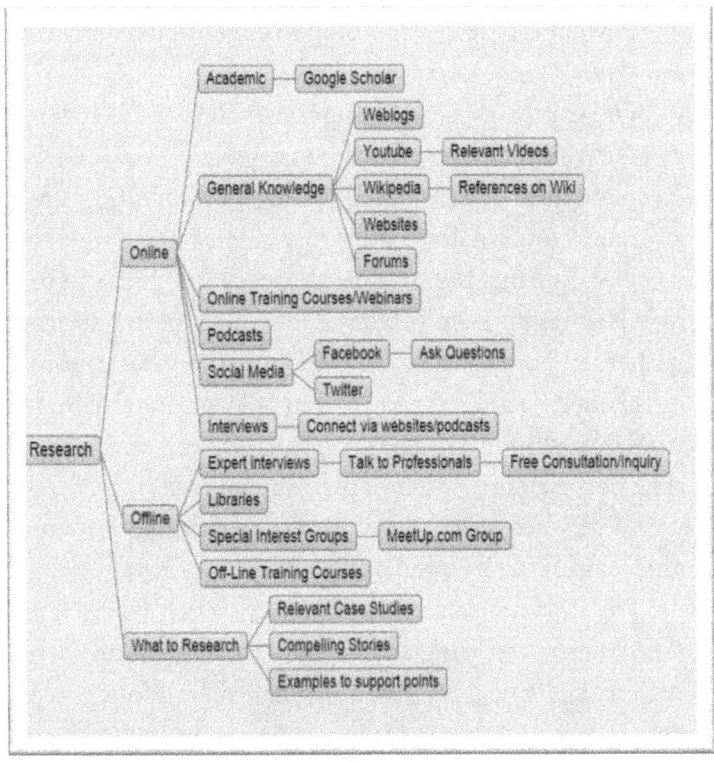

HOW TO DO RESEARCH SO IT DOESN'T FEEL LIKE YOU'RE DOING RESEARCH

Okay, so now you're ready to start doing research. You know why it's important, and what to look for, but how can you make the experience enjoyable and one that seems almost like a heavy burden has been lifted off of you? Well, that's what this section is going to cover in dynamic detail for you.

The first thing need to understand is that the approach is 'everything' when you're doing research. You don't want to spend a lot of time doing research for any long stretch of time. You also don't want to write for any long period of time. For this reason, this approach I'm going to teach you is going to keep you bouncing, but not in a bad way; rather, an enjoyable way in which by the time your book is finished you won't realize you're even done with your book. It will kind of sneak up on you and surprise you. The best part is it will be a pleasant surprise.

So let's get to it. I know you're wondering how to do this process, so let me share it with you.

The first step is you want to know what you're doing. This means knowing what you'll be researching, which means what chapters, subtopics, and subsections you'll be researching. So the first step simply means outlining your chapters so you have a holistic idea of what all is required in terms of content for you to get this book drafted entirely.

Try not to worry too much, at this point, about how to organize your chapters, subtopics, and subsections, because I'll be walking you through that in much greater detail later in this book.

The second step involves doing some actual research. When you're researching you'll be gathering both the information, and the bibliography citation for each piece of research material.

The third step involves taking a break from researching, and then starting some writing. When you are writing you'll be summarizing in your own words inside the same note on Evernote that you've placed your research for that chapter. The reason for this is you have all your research right in front of you, and now you can start formulating some ideas and summarizing what you think and how it applies to your books theme, and customize it to satisfy the benefits your readers want and expect from you. You always want to keep you reader in mind. We covered this in great depth in chapter 2.

After you've done some summarization on the research you've gathered for that particular section, then go back to researching again, only this time a new section.

You'll want to continue this process back and forth as you write your book.

The main thing to keep in mind with this approach is that you must not wait to summarize your research. The reason for this is because as you do the research and discover something new and insightful it is freshest on your mind. If you wait even a half hour you stand the chance of losing so much valuable recall from your memory.

I cannot express to you how many times I've done research and discovered something so valuable, only to wait a period of time and then come back to recall what I found was brilliant and find that I've totally forgotten everything. It would frustrate me when this would happen. So I caution you not to let the same happen to you.

HOW TO ACTIVELY ADOPT MY RESEARCH METHODOLOGY AND MAKE IT YOUR OWN PERFECTED METHOD

I think it is important to experiment with different models; that is, different methods to approach what it is you want to accomplish. For one, cycling back and forth between research and writing gets rid is the monotony of writing. It can become real boring doing the same thing over and over and over again. It's like swimming underwater and realizing you have no more air in the tank. You start to panic and become agitated. You start to suffocate and can't think clearly anymore. Nothing productive gets done when this happens during the writing process. You must come up for air every once and a while. It's natural for one to want to do this.

This is essentially the premise behind my method of operation when it comes to writing. I like to alternate between tasks, but 'strategically'. Now I realize there are some people who prefer to do all the research; compiling it, organizing it, and only then will they begin the writing process. However, I feel that an integrated writing approach works best for me. The reason is I have found in the past when I did all my research upfront that when it came time to sit down and write I found myself feeling fatigued and overwhelmed. I also noticed that sitting in my desk chair for an extended period of time writing caused me to think less and less about I should be writing. I became defocused. It would get to the point I would simply have to stop and go about my day without getting much done. I had lost my motivation to write, that is to say.

Something else, and this is worse than the aforementioned point I just stated, I would discover that most of the time I had spent researching intensely was wasted, because I would be skimming through a pile of research and would have forgotten where the various journal articles, etc., fit into the outline of my book. I had also forgotten what the research entailed. I was basically clueless. It was like starting from ground-zero all over again. This caused me to waste even more time and energy when it came to writing my book.

So I started experimenting and came up with this cycle approach where I would research a section, summarize the research so it made sense to me, and then later when I got into the real writing (I'll be teaching you this later, no worries!) nothing was ambiguous, and my course was charted perfectly so there was no guess work about what I should be writing. Everything made sense.

I want everything to make sense for you as well. In a situation like the commitment you've made to yourself today, where you'll be writing an entire book, beginning to end, what you want to do is maximize your efficiency, and I think the best way to do that for you, in terms of time, is to adopt this integrated approach of mine. You'll do some research, then write, do some more research, then write, and you'll continue this process throughout your journey.

When we get into learning more about the process of writing the book, I'm going to be teaching you some different techniques that are going to help you vastly speed up the process of writing. I'm also going to eventually, in another chapter, teach you how to edit your book swiftly. I'll be teaching you some shortcuts, but don't get it in your mind that these shortcuts I'll be sharing will detract from the quality of your edits, nor the quality of your book overall. Try not to worry, or get panicked at this stage of the game, for I assure you all this ambiguity will make perfect sense by the time you are finished with this book, and done with writing your own book.

For now just try and focus on the research aspect of this whole process. When you do some research and get some insights make sure you write down in a summary what the research comprises of and how it will benefit your reader. In other words, take the main points of the research and write it down as if you were telling a good friend what you discovered. You'd make it interesting; rather than, probably the boring dry stuff you found while researching.

If you think about it: You converse with an untold number of people each and every day, and during your conversations with people you tell stories all the time, whether you're aware of telling them or not. When you learn of something new, it's like something inside you compels you to want to share that information and news with other people. This is exactly the habit pattern I want you to form when writing your book(s). In time the activity of researching and writing come to you as easy as breathing. You don't even know you're doing so.

Remember your audience, i.e. reader, because these are the folks you'll be conversing with as you speak to them through the medium of your book.

Exploring new avenues and outlets, methods and approaches until you find the one that works best for you. Keep in mind writing is not a one size fits all approach. Everybody has their own approach they'll eventually adopt as their own method for writing books. By no means am I suggesting you adopt everything in this book; rather, simply take what's valuable and which makes sense to you and make it your own.

I have to assume that as you're reading my book, you're most likely reading other people's books. In fact, this book you're reading now has come about through my own personal research into various approaches adopted by other authors. Some of this you may find in other books; yet, much of it you will not. What's critical is that you find what works best for you. Don't think in terms of what I would do or what others would do; rather, think in terms of what will work best for you given your personal temperament.

Sometimes as we explore new ways of doing things we come across approaches that will slow us down, approaches which will make less sense to us, and approaches that we'll attempt and experiment with that we'll learn doesn't or does help us. This is okay. As you're continuing learning you'll evolve as a writer and learn through applying your own ideas and personal insights what is the best strategy to adopt for you.

Most of what I'm teaching you here has been discovered through applying what others have taught me and perfecting them until they fit my personal style and the way I like to work. I suggest you do the same for yourself. As you apply what I teach you, you'll find other things that are truly unique that perhaps one day you'll share with others. This is how processes evolve and become simplified and better.

I did not learn how to write a book in a flash my first time out. In fact the first book I wrote, though it only took me two weeks, still took me longer to write than any other book I successfully completed. Somewhere deeply embedded in my psyche was this belief that a book took nearly a year to write, in order to be any good. I have come to discover this is not the truth. My belief was wrong. In truth, the more I have written, and the faster I have rolled out books, those books have actually been of a much higher quality, possessing much more value. I think the more experience you get as a writer the better writer you become.

I personally get bored working on a project for too long a period of time. I like to get things done quickly; yet, I will not sacrifice of quality and value. So for me, writing a book quickly makes a lot more sense. If I were to make a commitment to write one or two pages per year until a book was finished I'd probably never get it completed.

I have to be completely committed and focused to get a book completed. I have to do this in the shortest period of time possible; elsewise, I lose all interest and start procrastinating until I eventually give up and quit. This is a pattern I've carried with me my whole life. In childhood I'd be interested in something and then a couple weeks later bored to tears with it and onto something else. It's the nature of change.

Because change happens, I think it is, at least for me personally, important to take action and see something through to completion before taking a different direction or doing something else. It is far too easy to get distracted sitting at a computer with the purpose of writing a book. You might find yourself checking phone messages, login into social media accounts, checking email over and over again—basically taking every detour away from writing. The problem is those detours hinder your ability to finish your book, and lessen the probability you will finish your book.

Imagine if you don't take the detours. What would happen if you took today and totally focused and got your book written, cover designed, ISBN assigned, and got your book files over to the printer, and tomorrow after having rested well, you realize you're a published author now? I'll tell you what would happen: You'd be thrilled to death excited, and all those benefits I mentioned in Chapter 2, they'd be on their way to becoming a reality for you in your life. My point? Take this writing business seriously, yet, have fun with it, and make it your own journey.

RECAP

In this chapter we sidestepped the clutter, which we'll be delving more into in future chapters relating to technology and software, as well as the writing process, and dug straight in to the research aspects of writing a book.

I shared with you some of the key secrets to doing research which shaves off a tremendous amount of time from the overall process of rolling out of your book. This is vital information to know-of if you plan on writing a book in a flash.

This information consisted of where to go in search of your research and specifically what to look for when you are collecting research materials. I also shared with you a tip in which you look for Wikipedia references and go search them out. Also I shared how YouTube is a powerful way to gain resources that are credible and which can explain and educate you very quickly on a particular subject just by enjoying watching a shore three or four minute video tutorial.

I also discussed with you the importance of alternating back and forth between researching specifically what you need for one section and then going and writing through summary form what you learned and gathered that would be of most importance to your readership. This was to prevent you from forgetting information or later not being able to distinguish what research goes with what part, or having to go back and reread research reports you'd already read once before. It also breaks up the monotony of writing, because one can quickly get drained sitting at a keyboard typing away for long periods of time.

The last thing we discussed was making your research method your own. You can take and test different approaches, including the one I've set out for you in this book, alongside others too, and find the magic formula that works best for you.

ACTION STEPS

Let me suggest that to the extent you do these exercises will be the extent you are successful in completing this program. By 'program' I mean that you'll finish your book in a flash, and not sometime way out into the future, or, heck, possibly never.

You want to succeed don't you? By that, I mean you want to get this book written now and out to market as soon as possible so you gain the benefits you're desiring from writing this book. Let me answer that for you: The answer is and emphatic: "Yes! I want to get my book written in a flash so I can enjoy the benefits of having a first-class book published and making me money well into the future which readers will love me for writing and gain tons of value from!"

Good! Do these exercises real quick and let's 'hop' to it, shall we? After all, we've got a book to get done in a flash!

I. Make a list of where you want to pull research from. This could be offline research methods, online research methods, or a combination of both. While you're making your list, think in terms of speed and efficiency. What methods are going to allow you to write your book in the fastest period of time?

II. Purchase the top three books in your niche and survey their table of contents to determine what is imperative you have in your own book. Use these books are references for the structure you wish your book to have. Also use them to decide how you might want to differentiate your book from them.

III. Start an Evernote.com account and create a new 'notebook' and start a new note for each of your proposed chapters. It's alright if you don't know what all your chapters will be named. Label each note: "Chapter 1 – Name of Chapter".

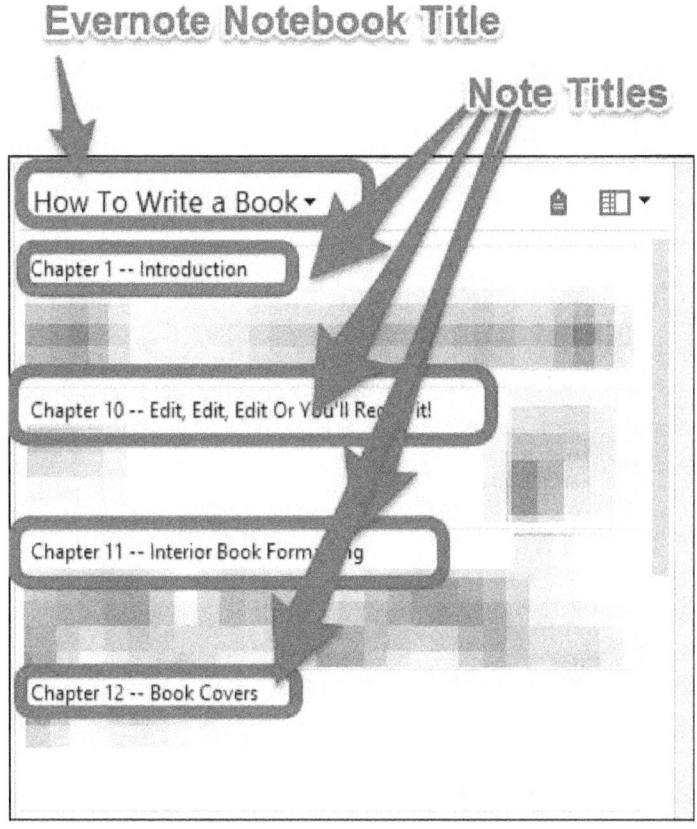

CHAPTER 3

TECHNOLOGY & USEFUL RESOURCES

Now that we live in the digital age, and technology is plentiful and constantly evolving faster than we keep up, I want to share with you some of the various technologies I use, and recommend you get, in order to write your book from beginning to end in a single solitary day, or at least done in a flash. I've used other technologies in the past, and I've used the ones I'm going to recommend to you, and I must admit that the technologies I utilize now, I wouldn't give up. They are dependable, easy to learn and use, and they save me a lot of time when it comes down to writing my books. Certainly there will be some readers reading this who will have a preference for using other technologies, and if so, that's fine. Just so you know how to use those technologies and use them as efficiently as I can use the ones I'm about to present to you in this book.

WHY IS THIS TECHNOLOGY VITAL TO YOUR ONE-DAY SELF-PUBLISHING EMPIRE

Many moons ago when I was in sixth grade I remember getting a writing assignments from my teacher Mrs. Armstrong, going home, sitting down with a pencil in my hand, and a notebook, thinking to myself, "Where in the world am I going to start?"

A deterring two page paper, double-spaced—so really only one sheet of notebook paper—seemed well beyond my capabilities. Whenever I submitted a paper and I received it back from Mrs. Armstrong, there were always red marks all over the place. It was in sixth grade that I learned proof-reading marks. This is where the teacher places these funny symbols that represent: insert a comma, new paragraph, delete this, insert something, and so on. Just seeing those bright red marks was frightening, even before I had a chance to learn what they represented. It sent a message to me, these marks, that writing wasn't an easy task. I had this belief I was going to have to work extremely hard in order to be a good writer.

When I reflect back on those days it is no wonder to me why so few people write books. The thought of writing a book for most people is a daunting one. It requires hard work, too much effort, tiresome research, boring edits where you constantly second guess yourself, there's formatting and cover design, not to mention ISBN's and all sorts of funny numbers and having to do a table of contents, index, author page, preface, forward, introduction, and so much more it seems to most people who even contemplate writing a book. Then in the back of your mind is the reality so few authors rarely sell enough books to break even on what it costs to write the book in the first place. The shelf-life for most books is well below 3000 copies.

To be a writer today in my opinion is much easier than my sixth grade experience of writing those two page, five paragraph essays. There are more people critiquing what I write, there's an audience of people reading my work, yet, today we have technologies that make writing a book so much simpler. There are editing programs that will literally edit your entire book for you. It only requires you to make the recommended changes to your draft. The software will even help you make the necessary changes. The software will also help you to improve your writing style, correct grammar and punctuation, even your sentence structures. There are also online plagiarism checkers to ensure you don't steal someone else's work inadvertently. There are article spinners which allow you to take your material and have the spinner software spin it using different words and phrases, while still keeping the meaning of your content intact. There is software that allows you to store notes, collect research, taking and storing pictures you take on a smartphone, take screenshots from off your mobile device and laptop or desktop computer. You can even record audio files using your smartphone and sync them into the notes to be retrieved later, when you actually begin the writing process. All of this wasn't available when I was in sixth grade; yet, it is today—it makes writing so much easier than ever before.

If you want to get ultra-fancy you can even purchase an audio recorder that records onto a microchip that can be inserted into your computer or smartphone to be edited later using other software. Such a recorder is pocket-sized and has the same if not better quality recording capabilities as what professionals use. The best part is these types of recorders can be taken anywhere you go, allowing you to instantly record any thought, idea, or insight that comes to you throughout your day, with just the touch of a button. In truth, you can write whole chapters of your book on such a tiny device to be transcribed later by yourself or a professional transcriptionist. It's really up to you.

There is technology out there that allows you to speak into a microphone and instantly the words begin appearing on the blank page staring you in the face. You no longer need a keyboard, or even a pencil or pen to be a writer anymore. You simply need your voice. To make your voice hear to the masses of people who might opt to buy your book you can speak your book's content, and later use the editing software, make any corrections you need to.

There's also the freelance route. If you need graphics, artwork, or even your whole book cover created, there are freelance agents who will be able to assist you at a very affordable rate. The online freelance marketplace has really grown over the years. There are so many people competing for your business that getting a good rate is usually no problem whatsoever. You can hire-out these freelancers to do ghostwriting, research, transcription services, videos to promote your book, editing services, and so on.

There are platforms and devices that are book specific—for example, Amazon has the well-known Kindle e-Reader. This device allows readers to purchase books from off the Amazon website and read them over their Kindle device, or even a laptop, tablet, or smartphone. The benefit of using one of the devices is that you can store entire libraries worth of books on your device and read any of the books anywhere you happen to be. This eliminates the need for people to have personal libraries in their homes these days. Personally, though, my preference is still to read a trade paperback over reading on an e-reader; however, I must admit I have and still do purchase books on my Kindle.

For this reason the advancement in e-reader platforms has made it mission critical for writers to make their books available through these sales channels. If you don't, you'll be missing out on a lot of revenue you otherwise would have captured. The good news is there's software out there that doesn't cost an arm and a leg to own, which automatically formats you print manuscript so that it complies with these platform requirements.

Word processing programs (e.g., Microsoft Word, Word, Word Perfect, Open Office, etc.) contain features now that they never did have in history. You can create a book index in minutes, without it being an all-day affair, you can create a table of contents for you book in seconds, and you can create styles for your headers and subheads to use just by clicking a button and watching the magic happen right in front of you, instantly. All of this makes it possible to write a book in a span of just one day.

If you're serious about writing and want to produce 'first-class' books, both quickly and easily, and in as little as a day, then you must have the right software and technology at your fingertips. I'll now be walking you through the technology and software programs and platforms I personally use when I write books.

WHAT SOFTWARE, TECHNOLOGY, AND DEVICES YOU WILL NEED TO WRITE A FIRST CLASS BOOK IN A SINGLE DAY—OR TO BE ON THE SAFE SIDE—A FLASH!

I'm going to run you through some of the software, technology, and devices I use to write books with little to no effort whatsoever, but books which are first-class and not mediocre by any means. These software, technology, and devices, will make your life 100x easier, if what you want to do is write books for a living. They will allow you to write your books in the shortest period of time possible so you can write book after book after book. In a few short days you'll have your first book listed on Amazon.com, the largest bookseller in the world, where people can access it immediately by buying it. The royalties from your books will be delivered to you in the form of a paper check, or if you prefer be direct deposited into your bank account.

The first software I recommend you owning is Eazy Paper. I'll list a picture below along with their website so you can get it now. Eazy Paper is a software I started using as a junior in college. It allows you to format papers in the major style formats (e.g., APA, MLA, Chicago, Turabian, etc.). You simply purchase a license to use the software, download it, install it, watch a short video tutorial on how to use the software, and you're done. There are two things I use Eazy Paper for specifically, when it comes to writing books; namely: (a) to create an instant bibliography/reference page for my book, and (b) to utilize two incredible features that are add-on features to Eazy Paper: The first is Eazy X-ray, and it allows you to scroll over any word, and find relevant synonyms and antonyms for these words. This is important because sometimes finding the 'right' word is difficult during the writing process, and because redundancy occurs frequently when people write. Redundancy happens because our linguistic patterns have become habits that are hard to change. For example, I use the word 'essentially' far too much in my writing. When I scroll over 'essentially' I find useful alternatives that I can replace it with—for example, words like: effectively, fundamentally, in the main, broadly, largely, more or less, to a large extent, in actual fact, principally, and trust me there's even more than these. In the main, you can get a sense of where I'm going with this bit on redundancy. We all have certain words we lean on more than others; that is, words we have become habituated to using over all the other words we could be using, and likely words that would be a better fit as it pertains to the context of what we are writing about. Using a wide vocabulary lets you present yourself as intelligent and well-read. Your writing will become instantly more eloquent, and you'll be perceived as really knowing what you're talking about. The second feature is the 'Hunt for References' add-on. It allows you to access libraries around the world, including the Library of Congress, and academic libraries, so that you can instantly find a properly formatted reference for a book you plan utilize during your research. You can also type in a subject and find all the books that are written about on those subjects. This can be a great way to quickly do research regarding book resources. I normally have the books already sitting on my bookshelf, but love this feature, because I don't have to pull out the book, look at the copyright date, the author's name, etc. etc. as I simply do a search for the book, and the citation is there for me to click a button, lickety-split and it's there at the back of my book, nicely alphabetized with all of the other sources. The software does this automatically. Its genius how this happens, considering I used to spend hours creating bibliographies for my books. Not anymore! You simply can't beat this feature.

www.eazypaper.com

The next software I use is the industry standard WhiteSmoke English correction software. Again, I'll list a picture for you to reference along with their website. WhiteSmoke is a writer's saving grace! As you do each section of your book, you can use WhiteSmoke to check your grammar, spelling, as well as find and replace instantly other synonyms that might be more appropriate. WhiteSmoke will also check for redundancy, and stylistic problems with your manuscript, helping you to write a cleaner, more polished book. The synonyms that WhiteSmoke comes up are not much different through-and-through from the ones that Eazy Paper's Eazy X-ray feature comes up with; however, that being said, I have found that when I cannot find the right word using Eazy X-ray, often I will using WhiteSmoke. Basically, you get more options to choose from. The nice thing about WhiteSmoke is that you can clean up your grammar and edit your manuscript as you go. This is not to say you might not want to run a grammar check again after your book is completed, running through it with a fine-tooth comb, so to say, because you'll definitely want to do just that. Still it does make it so that when you are finished writing your book that you'll have a draft copy that is clean and polished and for the most part correct and something you can be proud of.

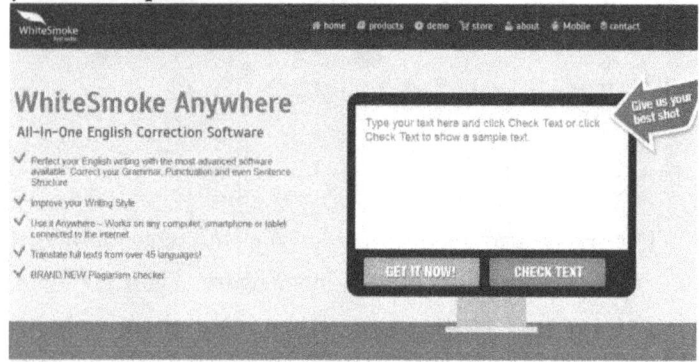

www.whitesmoke.com

The next software that I often use is a program called The Best Spinner. I've used other article spinning software in the past, however, The Best Spinner truly is in my opinion the best bang for the buck. If you don't like the way a paragraph or even an entire chapter for that matter reads, you can cut and paste your document into The Best Spinner platform, hit a button, and get a completely reworded version of your document. The Best Spinner uses language patterns and synonym variations to intuitively restructure your writing to make it something different.

Often time's writers complain they can't write what they want to say to their writers and it be easy to digest.

For this reason The Best Spinner comes in extremely handy. I've had periods of time when I couldn't come up with exactly what I wanted to share with my reader. I had the content. I even had the words down to be interpreted. The problem was the words I had written couldn't meaningfully be interpreted by the reader. When you write off-puttingly and convolutedly the reader has a painful experience trying to get through the noise in order to make sense of what it is you're trying to communicate. When I had moments like this when I couldn't find the right way to structure and sequence my sentences it could delay my book writing by days, weeks, even months. Using The Best Spinner I can change what I said to something that sounds more positive, intelligent, parallel, and easier for the reader to digest.

www.thebestspinner.com

Now you've heard me mention EverNote in the previous chapters. EverNote is a note taking platform I utilize whenever I write a new book, and throughout the entire writing of each book. It is one of the most valuable tools I have at my disposal and it is free to use. EverNote comprises of an online platform that has associated with it downloadable application software. What you do is visit the EverNote website, set up an account, and then download the desktop application for your laptop/desktop computer. If you happen to own an iPhone or an Android based phone, you can, and I recommend you do, download the EverNote app from either the Apple store or Google Play.

You can use EverNote either online or offline. What's nice is when you're writing a book often writers get stuck with this thinking that they have to write each chapter in order, before going on to write the next. This couldn't be further from the truth. When you're doing research for one topic you'll be writing about, sometimes you'll find content that would more appropriately fit under a different chapter. What I do, and recommend you do as well, is create one notebook in EverNote and name it whatever your book is tentatively titled. Then create inside that notebook a separate note for each of your chapters. I will label mine usually something like: **Chapter 1** – *Introduction*, **Chapter 2** – *Benefits of Writing a Book*, **Chapter 3** – *Fast Research Methods*, etc. Note that I don't necessarily name my actual chapters the same as I have them labeled in each of my chapter notes. As I get into my research or get to thinking about what might be a better title I will often times change the title. The purpose for having these chapters/notes all separated is that in EverNote all these pages are listed in order as they would be in my actual book when it gets written. As I'm doing research, writing down thought and ideas that come to me, or creating screenshot and taking pictures that will be included in the book, I can group relevant content in the chapter it will fall into in the book. This keeps everything nice and organized for me, and also I start to get a holistic sense of what my book is going to encompass. It also helps me determine when I have enough first-class content for each chapter. Having everything in order and summarized like it would be on an index card for each chapter, also gives me insights into what chapters I may want to exclude that might not make much sense being in my book alongside other content, or insights into what direction I should go in creating new chapters for my book.

EverNote has many great features which make your content look nice. There's an annotation feature where I can draw arrow to point out different attributes in a picture or screenshot. You can also draw shapes around specific content you want to draw out for the reader. You can also highlight content and even using a stylus freehand on your pictures and notes. You certainly of course can use another feature, the text writing feature, to write over pictures, and make notes within notes stand out vividly. You can record audio from either your laptop computer, or even your smartphone if you have the EverNote application, and it will store these files into your notes section. When we get into the actual writing process this recording feature can be very useful indeed. We'll be using

EverNote a lot today as you write your book, and I'll get more into how to use the recording feature in a later chapter. Another feature is the ability to screenshot content and save it in picture format to later be included into your book. For example, the screenshots I'm including in this chapter were all created using this feature in EverNote.

www.evernote.com

The next software is ExpressScribe. This software is a transcription software that lets you import an audio file and using a foot-pedal control the audio speed and be able to stop and start it whenever you need to. It makes it very easy and quick to take an audio recording you've created and turn it into text.

HOW TO WRITE A FIRST CLASS BOOK IN A FLASH • 69

www.nch.com.au/scribe/index.html

http://amzn.com/B009V62AMU

Next, I want to introduce you to the Zoom H1 Handy Recorder. This handy recorder is made Sound Laboratory Zoom in Japan. The H1 Zoom is a pocket size digital recorder that lets you record lectures, interviews, your personal thoughts, and even whole chapters of your book. This device produces professional sound studio quality recordings; making it possible to record high-quality content to later package and sell as a standalone product. You may even want to offer an audio version of your book, and this device would be a real asset in letting you do that in a way that produces the most value to your listening audience. The H1 Zoom also records in both MP3 format, as well as the higher quality WAV format. My favorite attribute this product offers is the ability to insert a Micro SD card into the device so you can record onto this small microchip, and then immediately transfer it over to your laptop for editing or transcribing purposes. The H1 Zoom only takes one AA battery and will record on this batter up to 10 hours of audio, before the battery will need to be replaced. I don't even go through one battery per book, usually, so just estimate you'll need one AA battery per book, and you should be in good shape. Incidentally, professional journalists use the H1 Zoom Handy Recorder to interview heads of state, presidents, and others because of the high quality recording capabilities this device offers.

You can also purchase a small lapel microphone that you clip on your shirt collar and plugin to your H1 Zoom. I usually use a lapel microphone with my H1 Zoom to speak out loud my thoughts and record my book chapters. I also use it when I'm giving lectures, keynote speeches, and when I'm doing workshop trainings around the world. Later I take the audios and repurpose them into books, or else edit them on my laptop and sell them on CD's or as MP3 downloads on www.indirectknowledge.com. If you do videos you can also record your audio track into the H1 Zoom and later go back and match it up with your video file and merge the two seamlessly. The quality is unmatched in my opinion.

HOW TO WRITE A FIRST CLASS BOOK IN A FLASH • 71

www.zoom.co.jp/products/h1/

http://amzn.com/B003VWC83Q

Another software I recommend is a program called Scrivener. This software is available for both Mac and Windows operating systems. It is much like EverNote in many regards, though it offers a much higher quality word processing functionality. Mostly I use Scrivener for writing fictitious novels over non-fiction how-to books. It is a great software that lets you organize your content, reorganize it as you like, and it integrates well with Microsoft Word and other major word-processing programs. Maybe my favorite feature is the ability to create an online index card for each section of your book. This keeps you organized and on point with your writing. When you have to develop a lot of character analysis and keep up with all the many elements that are crucial for writing a great work of fiction Scrivener is a writer's best friend. It can be applied usefully to non-fiction as well, and it also, like EverNote, will let you insert your research into your dashboard. This makes it possible to also do side-by-side research and writing at the same time. I really like being able to see my research next to my writing document. If you learn this program you may decide to forget about using EverNote, as both programs will serve your book writing purposes. Personally I use EverNote for my non-fiction and Scrivener for my novels. The primary benefit of both programs is that you can find what it is you're looking for easily without having to scroll down or up a huge word processing program. When you're in college or high school and writing a book report or research paper it may not seem like much of an inconvenience having to scroll up or down a few pages here and there. When you're writing a book, and have hundreds of pages to skim through it makes all the difference in the world owning these two programs—from an author's point of view. Everybody is different, however, so you may want to do things differently. However, I would rather give you more choices and options than try and limit you with only mentioning one platform. If I use it and love it I'll share it with you as well. Your opinion might be different than mine, and that's okay—customize these tools and resources to fit your individual needs.

www.literatureandlatte.com/scrivener.php

The next writer's resource I recommend you own is Dragon Dictation software. Dragon is developed by Nuance, Inc. This software lets you talk into a microphone and observe your spoken words magically begin appearing in your word processing program. It's 'talk and type' functionality at its best. You can dictate emails, social media posts, and even your entire book, using just this one piece of software. This is a great program for those who are slow at typing, have arthritis, or anyone who happens to be in a position for whatever reason that limits them from being able to type. In the early years of the computers similar programs weren't so efficient, however, Nuance, Inc. has seemed to get this software right, and for me, when I use it, it seldom makes a mistake. The software actually improves the more you use it, adapting itself to your speech patterns and voice tonality, etc. If you try it and it seems like more of a hassle than its worth, I recommend you not give up on it straightaway; rather, instead keep using it and learning about it, as it learns about you. It will get better—you'll grow to love it. Lastly, think of it like this: Top typists type 80 – 100 words per minute. The average human speaks 200 words per minute. So even being mediocre with this software will elevate you to a place above where many are who think only the best way is to simply type keys on a keyboard.

www.nuance.com

The next software I recommend is KD Publishing Pro. This software lets you take your print manuscript and format it for Amazon's Kindle e-reader. Many authors and publishers have complained about challenges they've had formatting their manuscripts so that they read well on Kindles and are acceptable for publishing by Kindle Direct Publishing, the arm of Amazon that handles Kindle e-book publishing. Using KD Publishing Pro makes formatting for Kindle super easy. You simply cut and paste your print manuscript into the KD Publishing Pro platform, and from there you can send it directly through the platform to Kindle Direct Publishing. This software will even make your chapters in your book hyperlinks, which is what readers prefer when they buy an e-book for their Kindle.

www.kdpublishingpro.com

Switching gears for a moment, I want to share with you some online freelance platforms that may be an outlet you'll want to call on from time to time for a litany of reasons. These platforms allow you to outsource jobs such as editing, formatting, graphic design, photo manipulation, accounting and bookkeeping, transcription services, online marketing and social media management, and virtual assistance for anything that can be done remotely and passed through the internet.

Here's my top 5 freelance list:

1. Freelancer.com

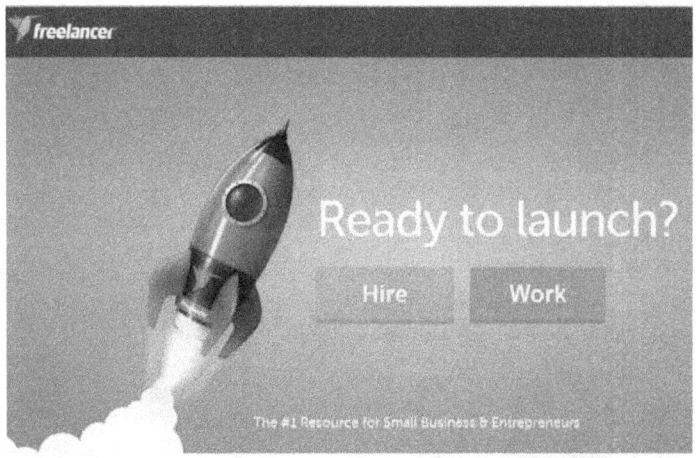

2. Fiverr.com

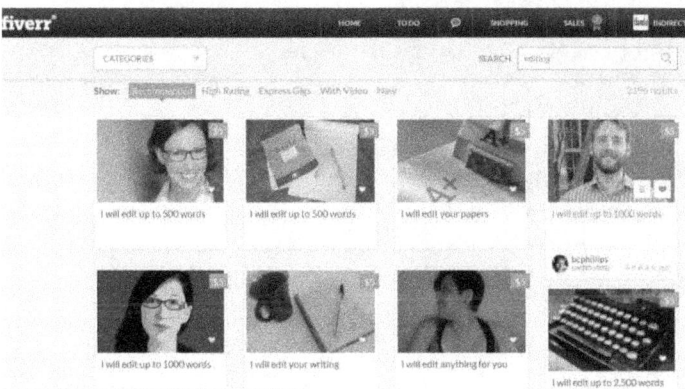

3. oDesk.com

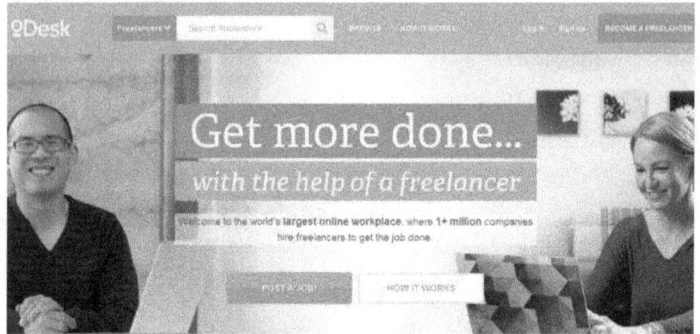

4. Guru.com

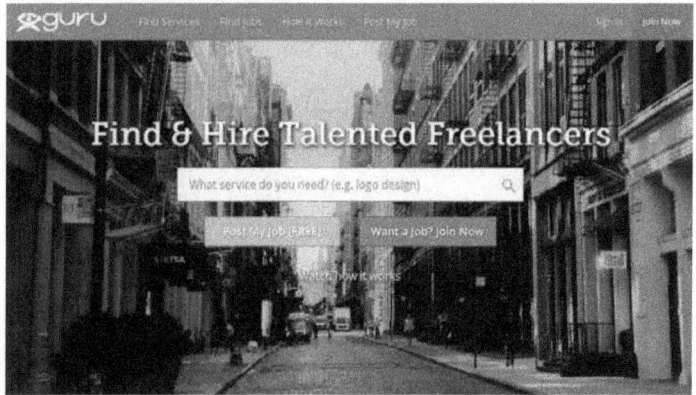

5. Elance.com

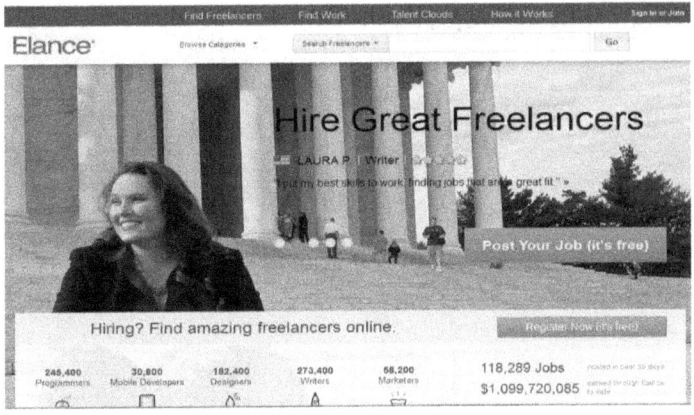

Remember, you can either become an outsourced freelancer, or hire freelancers to help you out in problem areas you're less predisposed to do extremely well in. Remember the 'reader' is your top priority. Everyone has different skillsets and you may be weak in a particular area whereas someone else may be very strong in that area of expertise. The final product you produce should be something that you're not only proud of, but more importantly a product that your customer will value and treasure holding onto and even recommend to their friends and family.

Hiring freelancers can really help with overcoming the workload of independent publishing—for example, with this book I hired someone to help with transcribing audios and even a fellow writer with a good reputation to write the forward for this book (I told you I would be completely transparent with you.):

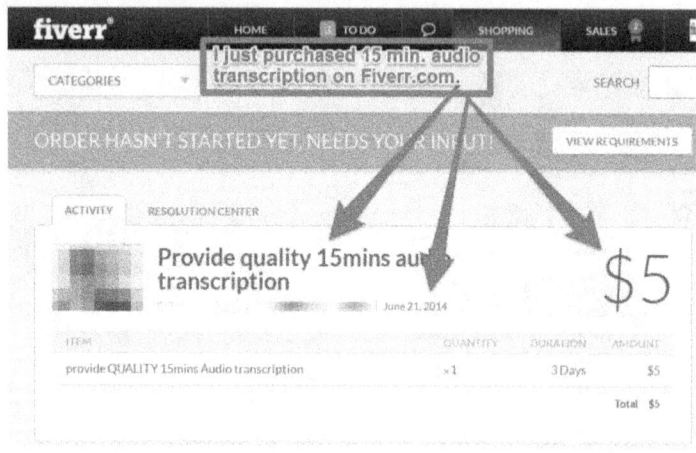

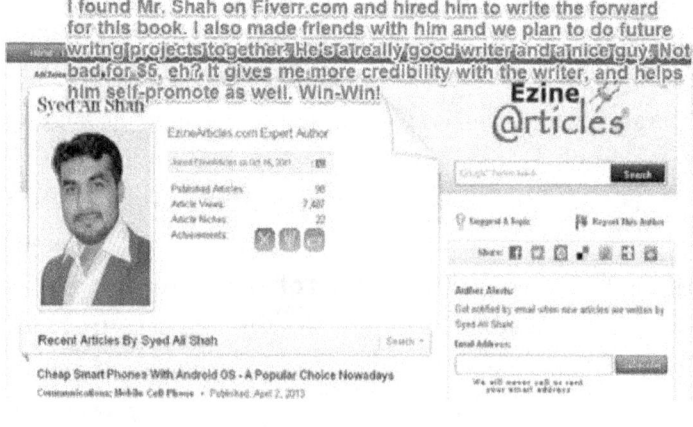

HOW DO I LEARN HOW TO USE THESE SOFTWARE PROGRAMS QUICKLY AND EASILY WITH AS FEW HEADACHES AS POSSIBLE

When I was in college I had a little situation that could have kept me from keeping my 4.00 GPA. I found myself in a classroom where the prerequisite was (I learned about this the first day of class, by the way.) to know how to use Microsoft Excel, backward and forward and even in my sleep. I may be going a bit overboard with the knowing it in my sleep, but the course was "Business Statistics" and, to be honest, I had very little experience with Excel.

The instructor told the class, "If you don't know Excel backward and forward, you'll fail this class, guaranteed!"

Imagine my heart stopping and my eyes jetting out of my eye sockets. I was paralyzed in that very instant—mortified! I had to have the class, and I didn't want to prolong my MBA any longer than I already had. I was getting a little long in the tooth to be romanticizing the idea of being a perpetual student.

Not knowing what to do I went online to YouTube and watched a series of videos people had created to teach business stats using Excel.

I remember it like it was yesterday, it was a Monday, I just walked out of class, and I found myself in the library, sitting at a private table, ear buds in my ears, focus entirely on the computer screen, watching away at those YouTube videos. At nine o'clock the next morning I was still watching those videos. I had my backpack packed with my laptop and gear, by 9:30, and by 9:45 I was back sitting in the same chair I had sat in the previous morning.

The instructor started talking about all types of statistical problems and randomly calling on people to answer her questions, without waiting for us to raise our hands, and to my surprise I was the only one in the class who knew the answers.

I nearly fell out of my seat and onto the floor when the professor said, "Class, Bryan, seems to be the only student in this class who knows Excel well enough to do well in this class. My advice to the rest of you is to brush up on your Excel knowledge. It is obvious to me that some of you will not be passing this class."

Sure enough, only three people passed her class, and only another girl and I got an 'A' in the class, and the other student didn't get a 'B'.

So why do I tell you this story? Is it to impress you with my knowledge of Excel or that I graduated with a 4.00 GPA? Most assuredly not! Hence what is the reason then and how might it be useful here in this chapter on technology and software and learning?

In order to learn how to use the different technologies, which I've presented you with, and that I personally use myself, first you're going to have to do some experimentation on your own. As a result you're going to have to do some testing, looking at some tutorial videos, and that's really what I want to talk about here. One of the best assets at your disposal, that's absolutely free for you to take advantage of, is YouTube.com. Most of the software programs I've listed for you to get have tutorials that other users have created, which are free of charge, and available to you completely online. Most of the software company websites have videos tutorials that the company has put out also. Consequently, you're in good hands in terms of how to use the software and get the most out of it. Even today I am still amazed at what I learn on YouTube.com that I didn't know about the software programs I own and have been using for years.

As it pertains to Eazy Paper there's a video tutorial on the software producer's website. Not all the features will be relevant for you in terms of writing a book in a flash, but the two that will (i.e. the bibliography creator, and Eazy X-Ray) are easy enough to master in a few minutes.

You'll be able to lookup sources in the Library of Congress and other libraries and instantly add them to the back of your book. Those sources you use which aren't there can be added by simply filling in a few blanks and clicking a button. The Eazy X-Ray synonym/antonym add-on is as simple to use as scrolling over any word in your document and waiting a couple seconds for a box to appear with a list that you can pick from which will automatically replace the original word in your document.

WhiteSmoke grammar and editing software is easy enough to use. It requires you only to hit the F2 key on your computer, after you've highlighted the text that you want to grammar check. Then, depending on which version of WhiteSmoke you purchase a box will pop-up and all your mistakes will be looking you in the face, with suggestions for correction. The software checks for style, punctuation, grammar rules possibly violated, spelling, and more. You then simply go through and make the appropriate changes. That simple!

The H1 Zoom Handy Recorder has several YouTube.com videos that will show you how to use the features and it only takes a couple minutes. The best thing about the H1 Zoom is that it is push-button simple.

There's no navigating screens or anything complicated about it. You turn the device on by sliding a button. Then when you want to record you press a big red button. When you're finished recording you simply hit the button again, and slide the slider-button again to turn the device off. You then transfer your data over to your audio editing software (e.g., Adobe Audition, etc.) and you're good to go. Mostly, I never edit my audios and instead prefer to slip them over to the Express Scribe Pro transcription software, through a simply upload button for instant transcribing. If you want to pay someone else to do the transcribing for you then you simply call on one of the freelance market places and find the best person to do the job that fits your budget. If you take this approach you will still be faced with having to go back and edit, or else outsource the editing of your transcript to some other freelancer. The choice is yours and the options are many.

Should you get stuck in your writing and find it difficult to make your sentences coherent you'll look to The Best Spinner software for helping you instantly spin your writing so it makes more sense, sounds more expert, and to help you produce the best product possible with the most value for your readership.

EverNote also has video tutorials to teach you how to use the platform. Most people I've interacted with tell me it's one of the simplest platforms to learn and one of the most useful. There are also other videos on YouTube.com that will walk you through how to use the program and take advantage of different features you may have questions about. Basically, you'll create a new notebook for your book, then create a separate note for each chapter in your book. As you compile research you'll slip it into each chapter (note) that corresponds to information you gathered. You'll also be able to use your smartphone or laptop to record audio files and slip those into each chapter. You'll also be able to insert screenshots, pictures, and other documents. As you write your book, you'll have everything organized, and it will be a simple process for you to turn all this you've compiled into a first-class book.

Scrivener is easy to learn as well. It is similar to EverNote in many ways, and it is fairly uncomplicated. There are YoutTube.com videos that will help you master the various features. Keep in mind that you'll really, for 'how-to' books, only need a couple of the features. You can learn these in a matter of minutes by watching some of the YouTube.com videos.

Dragon Dictation will take a period of time to master, but it isn't difficult. You'll be walked through when you set up this software how to use it and given information where to go to find the shortcuts to make using Dragon easier. Most of the commands are voice commands and make it so you never have to use your keyboard, but remembering all the shortcuts takes time to master. The more you use Dragon, the more you'll master this program, and the quicker writing using this software will be for you.

The last technology you'll need to know how to use is ExpressScribe. This technology is very simple to use. ExpressScribe is a transcription software that makes it simple to listen to an audio and type it out at whatever speed you're accustomed to typing. The software is used with a foot-pedal and the speed, stop and start, as well as being able to fast forward and rewind the audio when necessary is possible without you having to take your fingers off your keyboard. This makes typing out interviews and your book chapters easy and fast. This is another shortcut that makes it possible for some people to write a book in a single day. There are videos on YouTube.com that teach you how to use this software. Once you use it once or twice you'll have it down and become a fan of its features and functionality almost instantly.

Now you understand how I was able to have so much success in college. I simply discovered how fast learning could be when you utilized short, but pithy instructional videos on whatever topic I wanted to learn about. If you consider how much time is wasted when students have to get up, take a shower, get dressed, walk or drive across campus, find a parking place, walk up flights of stairs, find their classroom, retrieve their materials from their backpacks, and listen to the introduction from their instruction, and then sit through an hour long lecture, how inefficient sometimes learning can be. Why not instead learn something quickly in five minutes by simply watching a short YouTube video anytime that's convenient for you. It makes more sense to me to take this approach. And for this reason I suggest that you utilize this powerful strategy for learning how to quickly use the software I have presented you with here in this chapter. It will be possible for you to possibly learn these technologies now and still get your book written in a flash.

If you haven't purchased all of these software and devices you may want to do so as soon as you can. They will make your life a lot easier and it will save you a lot of money if you're planning to write multiple books in the future, and why shouldn't you—it's simple to write a book in a flash!

WHAT MIGHT BE SOME OTHER USES FOR THESE SOFTWARE APPLICATIONS AND DEVICES THAT YOU CAN USE TO CREATE OTHER PRODUCTS OR MAKE MONEY WITH

Once you purchase the various software I've brought to your attention inside this chapter, you will probably wonder what other uses you can use it for. For example, you can use Dragon Naturally Speaking dictation software to compose emails in a flash, without having to type them out. This can immediately save you time throughout your day, especially if you work in an office setting where you are constantly having to send emails.

You can use the H1 Zoom Handy Recorder to do interviews on the spot with anyone who is half-way and expert in the field you're writing about. You can then take these interviews and transcribe them and insert them into your book. You can also package the audio for sale on a website as a product and earn extra money this way, without having to do much else in the way of work.

Another great benefit to owning this software is by capitalizing on owning it by contracting out your services and expertise to other would-be writers or website and small business owners, by creating some freelance accounts on those earlier mentioned freelance websites. This can be a great way to learn how to use the software better, as practice makes perfect, but also be a great way to earn extra money. Personally, I think it is fun to help other people and I'm always learning something I didn't know which is expanding my range of skills to make my own business thrive more and me be able to work less.

If you decide to do some freelance work for others (this type of work in in abundance) you'll become a faster typist using the ExpressScribe software. It will make you so fast in fact that you may opt to stop using the Dragon Dictation software and prefer to record on the go (I record often when I take my dog for a walk) and later come back and type out what you spoke. I personally find this method easier and more enjoyable.

One thing I haven't mentioned yet is that you should also consider owning a subscription to Adobe's Creative Cloud Suite of products. You can get Adobe's: Premier Pro for video editing; Audition for audio editing; Photoshop for graphic and picture editing and graphic design work; and many more programs you can learn in your spare time. There are many video tutorials on YouTube and other sites that will help you master learning these programs as well. When you do master programs like these it will also open up many other freelance doors for you. You'll also have greater range of options as far as book cover design is concerned. Always be learning, that's my motto!

You can use EverNote not only for your book writing tasks, but also for storing photos to retrieve from any computer or device. You can create day notes to serve as reminders for you for every day of the week. Once you get into the functionality of how you can create such notes and how quickly the process is you'll find a lot of other ways even for which you might want to use this software.

So I'll leave it up to you to determine how you want to make money from these software programs, but you really do have a publishing house at your fingertips, all on your laptop. You have the ability to create digital products that can serve as online product launches for the different niches you work out of. If you're in personal development for example you can produce lectures and content that can be compiled in various digital formats and sold on sites like: ClickBank.com, LinkShare.com, ShareASale.com, JVZoo.com, and CommissionJunction.com. There are many ways today to make money online, if you own these software. Be creative and put your resources to work in your favor.

RECAP

Let's recap for a moment: First we looked at some of the various software programs; these included: Dragon Dictation, ExpressScribe, Eazy Paper, EverNote, Scrivener, and Adobe's Creative Cloud Suite (as an after-thought). Also, I mentioned you might want to consider owning a Zoom H1 Handy Recorder. And you'll need to purchase an Infinity foot pedal for your ExpressScribe software to function optimally. This is why I recommend you purchase bother together on Amazon.com and save yourself some money.

I then took you down the journey of what each software does and in what way you'll be using it today for the purpose of getting you book completed.

In the next section we dug-in a quite a bit deeper and I shared with you actually 'how' you can go about learning how to use each aspect of this expert product portfolio quickly and easily so as to jump ahead of the learning curve and master what you need to know immediately by utilizing YouTube.com to do so.

Finally, we went far beyond writing a first-class 'how-to' book in a flash using this software. We transitioned over to the bigger picture and discovered other ways this type of software might be useful in generating some serious income for you by taking up freelancing. Believe it or not a lot of professionals have left their corporate jobs to stay at home and to be able to do this they've turned to freelance marketplaces like the main five I've mentioned here in this book.

I think the quintessential key lesson here for you in this chapter is that in order to produce a book in a flash that is, shall we say a 'first-class' book, will require you owning some first-class software that will save you heaps of time. Leveraging your time by deciding to commit and get this software will benefit you in the not-so-distant future. The more books you can author (assuming you want to be a professional writer who writes all the time), the more money and sooner you'll be in that sweet spot to where you can literally do it full time and keep the lights on in your house (i.e., pay your bills and not worry about money and how you're going to survive).

It is sort of like being a newspaper writer. You're constantly spitting out new articles to be published. Newspapers have to have content, because buyers expect it, and papers run regularly, so content writers are constantly on their toes hustling to get the next story and get it to print before the next guy or gal does. Writing books has sort of turned into this same type of competitive landscape. You have to get something done and then get something going and continue repeating this process. It truly needs to be something you're passionate about, but also something that you take as serious as any other business. It's not all fun and games and to make money (at least enough to survive) requires that you keep the books coming. This process I'm teaching you will turn you into the newspaper journalist who is tasked with constantly putting something else out to market—only instead of a 500 word or less news article, you'll be writing 25,000 word books.

I very well may not be speaking to you however. I have to keep in mind that everybody has a different reason for wanting write a book, and many of you reading this will only be excited about writing one book and 'one' book only. If this is you, you needn't all these programs. You can simply get by with EverNote, in fact. The rest you can hire a freelancer to do for you, but it may not get back to you in a day, and thus writing your book may take several days—possibly still a 'flash' though! It's enough for you to write one book, some of you, so let's move on shall we.

ACTION STEPS

Let me suggest that to the extent you do these exercises will be the extent you are successful in completing this program. By 'program' I mean that you'll finish your book in a flash, and not sometime way into the future, or possibly never.

You want to succeed don't you? By that, I mean you want to get this book written today and out to market as soon as possible so you gain the benefits you're desiring from writing this book. Let me answer that for you: The answer is and emphatic: "Yes! I want to get my book written in a flash so I can enjoy the benefits of having a first-class book published and making me money well into the future which readers will love me for writing and gain tons of value from!"

Good! Do these exercises real quick and let's 'hop' to it, shall we? After all, we've got a book to get done!

I. Buy the technology and software programs I've asked that you get.

II. Visit YouTube.com and learn the essentials to each piece of software.

III. Peruse the freelance sites and discover the types of services each has to offer and pay particular attention to the rates being charged by the freelancers.

IV. Think how you might be able to leverage both the technologies and freelance marketplaces to help your writing process, and (if you like) earn some extra money to recoup what monies you've spent to purchase these resources.

CHAPTER 4

FINDING A SLANT TO PROFIT YOU AND YOUR READER

When you're writing your book you're looking for ways to differentiate it from your competition. Every niche has a market potential. This is the total number of people who are (for lack of a better word) into what you're writing about.

Quilters like quilts. In Paducah, Kentucky, not too far from where I live, there is an annual quilter's convention that takes place. Quilters come from everywhere around the world to show up and present their quilts, network with other quilters, talk about techniques, projects, and the stories behind their quilts—even how long they've been quilting. Some, I suppose, come to socialize and meet up with old friends they've known for years.

Sure these quilters have other interests, I'm sure. However, they all share quilting in common, and therefore they belong to the 'quilting niche'. There's a definite market for this niche, and therefore opportunities for capitalizing on other people's interests.

If you are a retailer who specializes in selling quilting supplies—for example: sewing machines, buttons, fabrics, quilting patterns, fabric rulers, thumb guards, needles, threads, and the like, then the quilters are your market. Smart marketers know their markets. They know about quilters. They types of people they are. What associations they belong to. Their primary and secondary demographics. They psychographics of the marketplace. They in turn use this understanding of their market to build 'goodwill' into the marketplace to position themselves as the 'go-to place' for quilters. They build their brand. They appeal to the market. They don't try and appeal to too broad a market. They get specific. They push their products out to the niche market they're operating within, because they know that this is where they're going to make their sales, and because they know this market inside and out.

When such a retailer builds an email list for this market they're sending out only marketing messages and promotional materials that are relevant to the market. They're not, in other words, for example, sending out emails about monster trucks and rodeos. That would be turning their back on the market. The market would react unfavorably (maybe make quilts with monster trucks or cowboys) and likely they wouldn't be interested in the promotion or offer being sent them. You see this is why it is important to understand and know your market, just as importantly as it is to know your topic and niche.

What you know and are passionate writing about likely has a market of people just as passionate as you are about the same exact topic. You know yourself, but you can still know yourself and what turns you on about your topic, and still miss knowing your market. It's not enough to know yourself, and believe other people feel exactly the same way you do. For this reason, a little market research is in order, before you write your book. This will also help you find your slant, which will help you differentiate yourself from your competition, and help you to build massive goodwill with your marketplace. They'll respect you for it. They'll love you for it. They'll profit. You'll profit. It is win-win for you and them—the way it should be!

WHY IS IT IMPORTANT TO KNOW YOUR MARKET AND HOW TO DO MARKET RESEARCH TO PRODUCE A FIRST CLASS BOOK PEOPLE WANT TO READ

Now that you know how to do fast research as far as finding relevant and up-to-date research to write your book quickly and easily, you also know, from purchasing the top three most current books on your topic from off Amazon.com or some other retail bookseller you know what's hot with your market. You know because you've read these books, and you know that consumers in your niche find what these other writers have written to be valuable and important. However, you cannot just write their books over again, or your market will call you out on it. If you don't believe me, just read some of the reviews from some of the other not-so-bestsellers in which their authors have tried to do exactly this. You'll see comments where the reader explicitly shares how this book is just a rehash of some other book that everybody in the niche has already read. This is a problem. Don't do you become tempted to do this. If you do, you'll get the same comments posted on Amazon.com about how your book is just borrowed material from somebody else's book. Nobody will want to read your book once they read these comments.

This being said, once you read those other author's bestselling books, you'll gain some valuable insights into your market, and what makes them get excited, and what makes them tick. This is really more valuable than you might realize, because if you know your market, and you know what makes them tick, you can come up with new content; that is, a new slant, which predictably will have a similar impact on them, and in turn create massive goodwill with your market, as these authors have already achieved.

Now what you're probably wondering is how do you come up with a slant that makes this impact? We'll get to that in a minute. First, I want to call your attention to something else.

Why else market research is important has to do with the fact that people want to buy what they want. I know. I know. This sounds really grade-school rudimentary;

however, you would be astonished to learn how many business owners and product launch experts completely forget this vital building block. If you know what people want to buy, doesn't it make sense to sell them what they want, instead of what you want to sell them? I think so. And, most other people agree with me.

But you say, "What about the people who don't know what they want?" Good question. There are a lot of indecisive people out there. They tend to be the followers who want what everybody else wants. So the same rule still applies. Give people a product (in this case a book) that most of your market wants, and those people who are indecisive about what they want, who are still a vital section of your target market, will follow suite and purchase your product also. This gets into consumer behavior and consumer psychology, which is outside the scope of this book; yet, you still get the point as to why it's important to do your market research and find a slant that will elevate you up on a pedestal in front of your primary market.

The last point I want to make in terms of why you need to give your market what they want, which means certainly doing your market research, and finding a unique slant that will appeal to your market, is because if you give your market what they want, they will be your best publicists. That's right, when one person finds your book refreshingly original and desire some, they'll share your book with their peers, which most often are people with similar interests; that is, your target market, and they'll tell their friends, and sooner or later everybody is telling everybody about your book, and now your books gone viral, and is selling thousands of copies. So now you know why this is vitally important to get right, before you go and launch a book nobody wants, and those who happen to buy it despise and possibly hate you for. And, probably hate themselves for buying.

WHAT DO YOU NEED TO KNOW ABOUT MARKET RESEARCH AND FINDING AN ANGLE FOR YOUR BOOK THAT MAKES READERS WANT TO BUY IT

Getting back to the question I raised for you a moment ago: How do you come up with a slant that makes an impact on your market to make your target market want to buy your book? This question starts us down the road to doing market research. The first thing you need to know is what your market craves. What makes them thirsty for knowledge? Why do they care about this niche? Most of the time when you ask somebody why they like something they say, "I don't know. I just do." Obviously it has some type of meaning to them—some type of value—something that attracts them to the niche.

I knew a man once who had an obsession with owning church pews. He had a big family, and a big house, and throughout his house were church pews. When he invited me over and showed me his obsession I was taken aback. I had never met anyone before who had a church pew in their home—let alone several. It sort of shocked me and created a curiosity inside me that made me ask him, "Why church pews?"

His answer shocked me. It will you too.

You see, the man took quite literal the saying, "A man's house is his temple." This was his answer, after first telling me, "I don't know. Why not?"

Later I learned, after building some rapport with him, that throughout the week the man held Bible classes, in his home, where he taught people from his church, and anyone else he could get to come, about the Bible. In fact, this man had an even greater obsession with memorizing the entire Bible from beginning to end. He was devoutly religious.

Now why did he have church pews in his home? It was because he had an internal need to associate his home with being a place of holiness and reverence for his beliefs in his god. It made him feel closer to his god, and that was important to him. It also gave him a higher sense of purpose, which held some intrinsic value for him on a personal psychological level.

Why do I share this story? Because, it illustrates the point that on the surface when someone give you an answer it may be very logical, well-reasoned, and maybe simply the easy way or the, "I don't know. I just do." On a much deeper level, asking thought-provoking questions, you can learn the deeper reasons, which often more are emotionally associated with their behavior and why they're attracted to the niche that they're attracted to.

So what you first need to know is what how to question your market. It involves surveying the marketplace to determine what people are in need of, what they want, and what they perceive as urgent in terms of what their market needs holistically.

Some of the best product launches were designed without a product even in existence. In reality, these same successful product launches because successful launches because they first did the market research to find out exactly what their market wanted. They did surveys. Built email lists. Gathered potential, and even likely customers, long before they even had a product to sell. I know one person who told me he didn't even have a website for his product until the day he launched it to his marketplace. He then shared with me that he gathered more than twice as many emails the week he launched his product, than he had gathered in the nine-months leading up to the launch. This is because his marketplace loved his product and it went viral and word-of-mouth spread like wildfires.

I would encourage you to buy some other books specifically on market research, as this book will not take you into much detail whereas market research is concerned. There are MBA programs literally dedicated to teaching business professionals how to o market research. It's a huge field, and this book is not intentioned to take you there, because, candidly speaking, the day would be over and your book wouldn't be written. You bought this book because you wanted to learn how to write a first-class book in a flash. Let me stay on point with exactly that while encouraging you in the future to do some self-study on market research.

In terms of finding a slant you need to be able to dissociate yourself from yourself, and be able to put yourself in the shoes of your potential customer, i.e. reader, but also people who are not your target market who might for whatever reason might buy your book.

Remember those reviews on Amazon? You know the ones with 149 five star review and 5 or 6 one and two star reviews? Who do you think comprise the people who left the one and two star reviews? That's right—it was the people who bought the book who weren't the market. I mean have you ever bought something and later asked yourself: "Why did I buy this?" Well, other people do the same thing, and when that buyer's remorse or what social psychologist Leon Festinger might call 'Cognitive Dissonance', happens, we like to blame somebody; whether it's the guy that sold you the car that wasn't the one you really wanted, or the author that wrote a book with a title that seemed intriguing until they started reading what it was actually about—that's right the author takes the rap and gets the one star review! Boohoo. Poor me. Why did they have to buy that book in the first place? Who knows, but had you prepared in advance for the possibility someone might buy your book who wasn't truly your market, you'd maybe have taken some precautions to market it better so as to create less ambiguity for buyers.

I wrote a book once and received a phone call from my nephew. The book was on a subject relevant to my niche. I wrote it for a specific market. My nephew had seen the book and saw the price was $20+ and had to tell me how he would have bought a copy, but that he thought the price was way too high. He couldn't believe I would price it that high.

Knowing him, like I do (we're a close family), I asked him: "If I had written a book about 100 secret martial arts moves that could instantly kill a person, and priced it at $49.95, would you have considered buying it for that price (martial arts is his thing)? He paused, and said, "Yeah, probably, but…" I cut him off at 'but', and simply said to him: "You are not my market." You won't hurt my feelings if you don't buy a copy. You are not the person I created the book for, and so of course it doesn't hold the same value for you as it does my target market. The book did well and sold a lot of copies, and I never changed the price. My nephew never bought a copy either, which I knew of, and that's okay by me.

This story illustrates the importance of knowing your market so well that you can read them like a book (no pun intended). If you can read them so well, then you can write a book that they will read well too. It's about giving them value and what they want, and this is what you need to know about market research and be concerned with in regards to a basic understanding of the subject.

HOW TO FIND A SLANT FOR YOUR BOOK AND STEP INTO THE SHOES OF YOUR TARGET MARKET AND INDIRECT READERSHIP TO COVER ALL YOUR BASES

You've started thinking about your target market. You think you have an idea of what types of people make up your market and what draws them into the marketplace for they type of book you'll be writing. The first thing I want to teach you is a simple Neuro-Linguistic Programming (NLP) exercise to help you read (pun intended) your market, better. It's called Perceptual Positions.

A perceptual position is stepping into a point of view (could be your own or somebody else's). In NLP there are three perceptual positions. They are: (a) first position, (b) second position, and (c) third position.

In first position you are assessing how someone feels, thinks, observes the world, through your own eyes from your own model of reality. This is the position we're naturally in all the time. When you're excited about a new product or book that comes out, in first position you assess your feelings and analyze this behavior from this perspective.

In second position you are assessing how a potential customers, i.e. someone else interested in your book feels, things, observes the world, by literally pretending to step into their shoes and become that person (imaginatively speaking). You start to play around in your head with how you feel being that person, how you're thinking being that person, and you pretend to understand the world from their model of reality.

In second position you really start to understand your market by becoming them. You start to learn, from their perception why your book is important to them and why it is not. You also start to conceive how they plan to use your book in their own life. You also start to contemplate their behavior patterns, values, past, and so on; in order to get inside their head and make predictions about how they will perceive your book as being.

Let me share with you why this exercise is so important. I had written a book once and it was finished and on Amazon, making some sales, and I got a phone call from Jennifer (my significant other) who had been on vacation visiting her mother in Michigan. Her father, who lives in Dayton, OH had actually driven down picked her up and he was visiting up in Michigan also.

I instantly picked up the phone when I saw that it was Jennifer calling. The reason for her call kind of caught me off guard, however. She told me her father was interested in one of my books. She also asked me to send a copy out to his address in Dayton. Of course, I agreed.

When I got off the phone, I was not really nervous, but felt a little uneasy that someone I knew and respected would be reading something I had written. I had never really considered her father my market, but looking back on it I suppose he did fit into that target marketplace.

I was thinking all sorts of thoughts—for instance, what if he doesn't like it, or what if he thinks I'm an idiot, and so on. I know this sounds a bit paranoid, but it will happen to you, more than likely, when you find that someone you know wants to purchase a copy of your book and will seriously be reading it. I call this day: *Judgment Day*, because it's one thing to get some perfect stranger critiquing and judging your masterpiece, yet it's an entirely different situation when you have someone you know and respect judging it.

My reason for telling you this story is not to scare you; rather, to let you know that if you'll put yourself into the person of someone who is likely to buy your book and be reading it (better is someone you know personally), then you'll write a better book, and you'll write it more for them and less for you.

Third person perceptual position is when you literally step into the shoes of an 'objective' observer—someone other than your market, yet someone who knows you've written a book on the topic. By taking this person's perception you imagine what someone who isn't your ideal readership will think about your book. This person is indifferent to your book, to you, and possibly has bought the book without really knowing why. You start to assess what kind of review this type of person might leave you, and by that I mean you start to contemplate what someone non-biased nor attached to your book would think about your book.

In this way, taking this third position, you will start to understand what someone like my nephew thought about my book, when he called me up and told me it was overpriced. He wasn't my market, yet, he still had a perception about my book. You want to know what these objective observers think so you can write a better book and get these people not being overly critical of your book, but rather helping you promote it and tell other people about it. For instance, I know, having done this exact same exercise, that my nephew, if he comes across anyone who fits into my market, will share knowledge of my book with them and encourage them to buy it. He knows I put out high value books, but he also thinks they might be priced a little too high. To the market, having done the second perceptual position exercise, I know they'll see past the cost, and see mostly only the value. From my own first person perspective, I know that the value is definitely there and that I'd be fine with people I personally know purchasing the book and learning what I have to teach.

I hope when you read about that story I just now shared about Jennifer's father, and reading my book, it shocked you, or that you imagined this type of thing happening to you. It will eventually, so it's best to write a book that is something all parties will judge favorably (i.e., you, your targeted reader, and any reader who happens to read your book for lack of a better reason).

Now that you have considered all the perception of people who might be reading your book (and probably will be) the second thing I want to teach you is how to find a unique slant. To do this I want to introduce mind-mapping. This is something I do with all the books I write. It is simple to do, there's even great software out there that allow you to do it to, but there's also something to be said about taking out a sharpie marker and a notebook and mind-mapping the old fashioned way. I do both, and I'll be sharing my process with you, in case you find it is helpful to your process as well.

Mind mapping is important because it gives you a holistic perspective of your topic, and allows you to chunkdown into specifics that start to help you brainstorm and form the ideas which will become your eventual book. Mind-mapping helps you start to organize your content so you know exactly what you need to research to be able to write your book. It saves you a lot of time, because it prevents you from doing broad research on things you won't be putting in your book. There's no point in spending a lot of time researching aspects of your topic that you don't intend to write about.

What is mind-mapping? When I was in eighth grade I had an English teacher named Ms. Wooly. I know that's an interesting last name! Ms. Wooly though, one day, passed out to my entire class a book on writing. This was when I first learned about mind-mapping, even though in this particular book it was called something else. It was actually called 'bubbling' and 'webbing'. Today, it's come to be called mind-mapping, and who'd of ever thought that I would be utilizing a brainstorming technique I learned in eighth grade (back in the early 1990s) to be professionally writing books today. I guess it just goes to show that nothing's ever wasted.

Mind-mapping begins with a central topic which you label in the center of a piece of paper, and draw a circle round (or bubble). From this central idea you start to down-dump everything you know about this topic into subtopics. Each subtopic you circle and draw a line to from the main topic—connecting them. This starts to form what sort of looks like a web (thus why they called it webbing). From the subtopics you start to down-dump everything you know about each specific subtopic to for a sublevel off of each one of these subtopics, and you start to draw lines connecting the sublevels to the subtopics. You can go even deeper than this if you want, until you exhaustively put down everything you know about your topic, subtopics, and sublevels.

Once you've created this mind-map you then start to use your critical thinking skills to determine how you can differentiate your book from your competition. This is rather easy to do since you can simply look at the table of contents of the top three books and see what's missing that you feel would add a lot of value to your readers' understandings of your main topic.

It is important to note that a lot of what you add into your book will cross-over what's been written about by these other authors, and some of it will be necessary for you to include in your book. For example, you may notice some patterns emerge from the top three books; namely, that they all have a 'history' chapter explaining how your topic came to be. This would be useful to have in your book also, given that some of your readers, many of them in fact, may be reading your book as a first book on the subject material. Knowing the history of your topic would be useful for them. Other topics may be discovered to be repeated in the table of contents of the top three best sellers you'll be referencing, and, again, you'll have to make a decision if it makes sense to discuss these chapters and sections in your book as well. Remember, you can always put a different spin, or add a different flavor, when you do include these sections in your book. The key is to make them interesting, yet distinct, so your reader's who've already read these top three books, will get a different perspective and find value in re-covering this material, without getting bored or agitated. You can use your creativity to help you do this.

Here is an unfinished copy of the mind-map I started for this book. I ended up finishing this mind-map later-on, on my computer using mind-mapping software from www.novamind.com.

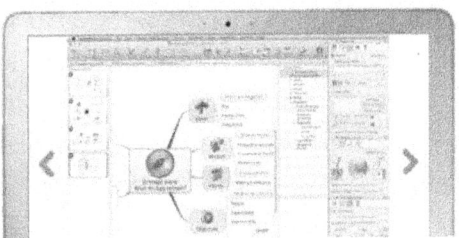

Here's the mind map I did on my notebook using a Sharpie maker:

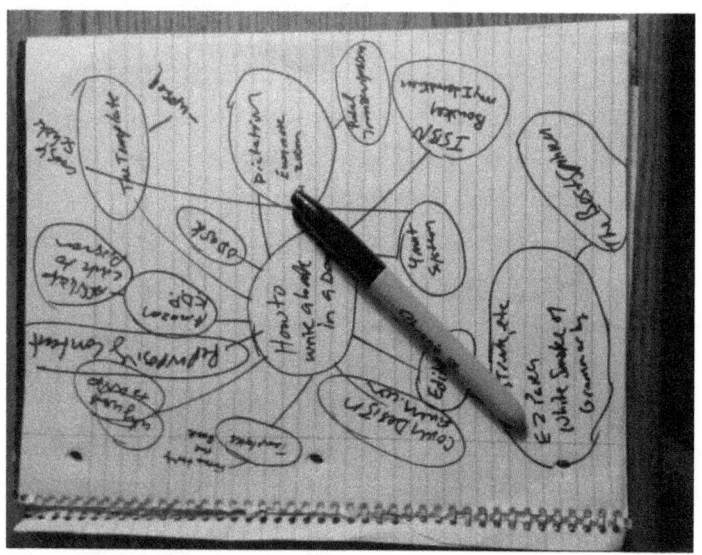

Notice how some of the sublevels may well fit under multiple subtopic categories. Notice also that the main topic (center circle), is not the title of my actual book. I didn't have a title for the book at this stage of the game; rather, I just had an idea for a book I wanted to write. Notice also that not all of the subtopics became chapters in this book.

You see, the subtopics are just brainstorms which guide you toward possible ideas as to what your chapters will eventually become named. Once you've completed your mind-map and are satisfied you've exhausted every possible idea; and by the way, many of these ideas come from what your market has told you they want. This is why you'll also want to do quantitative market research like surveys and Likert scales, and also qualitative research like interviews and observations (e.g., looking at the table of contents of your three top competitors, etc.) to get a clearer understanding of what your target market expects, wants, and needs from your book. When you're creating a product you always want to talk to your market to determine what they want. We're writing the book for them primarily.

So once you have all of these things exhausted, it's time to make some decisions about how you can make your book stand out; that is, "What's your slant?" A great way to decide your slant is to look at your subtopics in reference to your main topic, and determine what hasn't been written about before, but which if you wrote about, would appeal to your readership. This can also be useful for narrowing down the scope of your book to write about something more specific. Originally, and I haven't included the picture here, because I no longer have the original mindmap, my main topic was: 'How to write a book'. One of my subtopics was 'book in a day'. Another was 'first-class book people wanted to read'. I narrowed down this focus to determine that I wanted to write a book about 'How to write a first-class book in a flash'. There were two bits of market research that helped me determine this was the best slant for my book: (a) I had read on an Amazon comment from readers who had read other authors books who had written on 'How to write a book in a day' that that indicated that the authors took shortcuts which caused concern for the market that writing a book in a day would detract from quality and the value the market expected. So this led me to add in the bit about 'first-class book', and I got rid of the 'day' part, thinking people would be more receptive to 'flash' instead—a word that's more ambiguous and less promising. (b) I had visited http://www.google.com/trends and looked up keywords relevant to my book project to determine which were trending and which were not. For example, I looked at keywords like, "how to write a book in a week', 'how to write a book in a year', 'how to write a book in a day', and I noticed the trend leaned favorably on 'how to write a book in a day'. Then it was just a matter of deciding how my book might be perceived by my market and other people who might purchase my book. For this, I used the NLP perceptual positions exercise, I shared with you earlier. I finally made the determination that my slant would be: 'How to Write a First-Class Book in a Flash'. It satisfied those who thought that writing a book in a day meant losing quality, and it corresponded with the keyword trends of those in my marketplace (most likely you) who wanted to write a book in the shortest period possible. I still wasn't comfortable making the promise that everyone who wanted to could write a book in a day, because I haven't met everyone, and though I can write a book in a day, and have, I thought it best to use 'flash' instead. Flash still lent itself to being fast enough! A flash could be less than a day, or it could be several days, and so it worked.

Then once I had my slant, I started zeroing in on what was necessary that I include in my book, and what was secondary. At this stage, you'll want to take your mind-map subtopics and rank-order them in terms of importance. Then decide what is necessary and what is likely to detract from the quality of your book, and this is how you come up with your chapters. Keep in mind, these have already been predetermined in terms of importance by your market, when you did your market research (surveys, etc.). Don't think it's what you necessarily think is most important; rather, it's what your target market believes is important. Use good judgment though.

Earlier in this book I talked about the importance of picking a certain number of chapters and sticking within those guidelines. This will help ensure you make good decisions about what you include and don't in your book. Remember, you're placing imaginary limitations on yourself, because you don't want to use filler and what's been called by most people as 'fluff' to pad your book to make it thicker. By now, you're beginning to realize there's a lot more quality content out there to fill up a million pages. You never have to think you have to fill up your book with fluff just to make it thicker and appear to have more value. Your readers will hate your for this and you'll know this by the negative comments they leave you on Amazon.com. Just don't do it. You don't have to.

Once you do decide what will be your chapters, and you have your slant, and things are starting to make sense mentally in your head, and what was once just an ambiguous idea is now becoming more and more a fixed reality, it's time to develop your chapters, as you did your main topic, by mind-mapping them too. Let me say, however, that you may not have to mind-map ever single chapter, as you may have mind-mapped enough on your first mind-map to have enough information to do your content research on. Some chapters, however, may need more development, and if this happens to be the case, mind-mapping will greatly help you. Here's a sample mind-map, using NovaMind software that I did for Chapter 3 of this book. Incidentally, I knew a great deal about how I do research, yet, still, I didn't know how best to organize it for you guys and gals reading this book. The mind-map saved me a lot of time and gave me a clear direction to be able to present my quick-research methods to you all in a nice way:

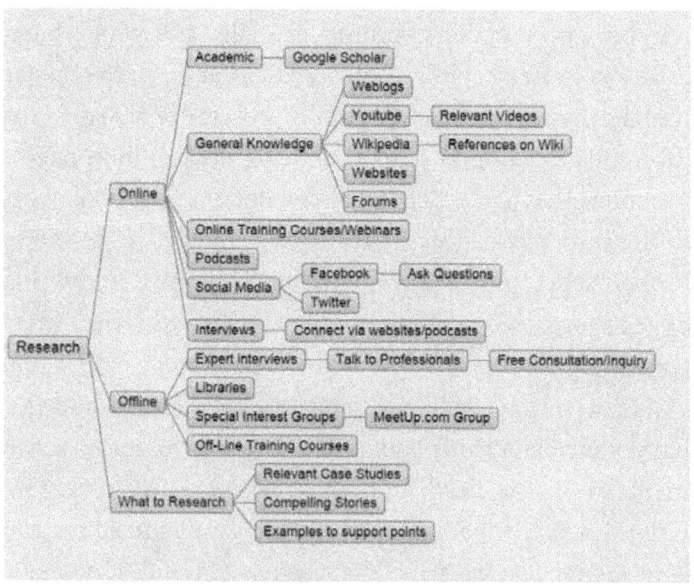

Now you have a clear direction of how to find a slant for your book. Of course, don't restrict yourself, entirely, to my process; that is, use what's useful, and leave what's not necessary for you. Also, I always encourage writers to adapt what I teach to suite their own learning style. You very well may find other great ways to get to the same ends, and if so—wonderful!

The final point I want to make is that your subtopics will guide what you'll name your chapters. Your sublevels off of these subtopics will guide what you'll include, i.e. the various sections, in each chapter. Your research, then, will be focused only on these subtopics and sublevel topics -and, organized accordingly into EverNote, Microsoft One Note, or Scrivener (depending on your software preference). Once you have your research completed and organized you'll begin writing your book based on your research, thoughts, and expertise.

THINKING PAST THE SYSTEM TO CAPITALIZE ON TRENDS TO MEET MARKET DEMAND WITH PRECISION PERFECT TIMING

You may recall, I mentioned how I utilized Google Trends to identify market demand. If you keep a blog on your topic, because it's your passion, and probably all you have the desire to write about, or because you want to position yourself as a leader in your niche, then you can utilize the Google keyword generator tool to find what is ranking highest in terms of Google Search entries. Actually, you don't even need your own blog or website, though it's nice to have one, because you can actually use someone else's.

To do this use the Google keyword generator, which will tell you what keywords are pulling up a particular website (e.g., your website). Pick the keywords relevant to your book topic that make the most sense. These will be keywords that are getting the most searches on Google. Once you determine which keywords are being searched out the most, look on www.google.com/trends to determine if they're poised for growth and are trending or if they're declining in popularity. Also, pay attention to various trending patterns. Some topics are searched more at various times of the year—for example, 'retail' is hottest during the Winter holidays, and not so much in late January and February. You'll be able to tell this by looking at the times when the keywords are trending up versus when they're trending down. Obvious patterns emerge for some topics, whereas less obvious ones emerge from some others, which you have to use a careful eye to spot. Knowing this information can also help you spot 'sweet spots' in the market which will tell you the best times to launch your new book. Keep in mind, you want to capitalize as much as possible from your new book, because it will not be new forever, and other books will be written which will compete for buyer's attention. Many book readers look for newly released books. So make your launch date count, and take advantage of market trends.

RECAP

In this chapter I walked you through the importance of doing proper market research and finding a distinct slant for your book. I also taught you how to use NLP perceptual positions to head-hack your target readership as well as others who might decide to purchase your book and read it.

I covered the importance of mind-mapping to decide your slant, but also to determine your specific chapters, and the subheadings you'll be including in each chapter. I taught you how this will help you know explicitly what to research to save you hours and hours off your research time. Knowing what to research is just as important as knowing how to do research quickly and efficiently (we covered this in chapter 2).

I also taught you how to use powerful online market research tools; namely: Google's Keyword search, and Google Trends, in order to monetize your book to full capacity and share with your readership what's important for them to know now, while it's a hot topic.

By now you're beginning to understand how possible it is to not only write a book in a flash, but also how possible it is to write a 'first-class' book in a flash.

ACTION STEPS

Let me suggest that to the extent you do these exercises will be the extent you are successful in completing this program. By 'program' I mean that you'll finish your book in a flash, and not sometime way out into oblivion, or possibly never.

You want to succeed don't you? By that, I mean you want to get this book written in a flash and out to market as soon as possible so you gain the benefits you're desiring from writing this book. Let me answer that for you: The answer is and emphatic: "Yes! I want to get my book written in a flash so I can enjoy the benefits of having a first-class book published and making me money well into the future which readers will love me for writing and gain tons of value from!"

Good! Do these exercises real quick and let's 'hop' to it, shall we? After all, we've got a book to get done today or rather a flash, that is!

I. Take a few minutes to do the NLP Perceptual Positions exercise. Write down the critical differences you'll need to address in your book to ensure your book receives rave reviews, remains first-class, and communicates to your target market amazingly well.

II. Make a mind-map of your books topic. Do not over think the process. Simply down-dump everything that immediately comes to you about your subject. From this determine what slant you want for your book and what your chapter headings will be for your book. Be careful and make sure you compare your mind-map to the table of contents of your top three competitors. They may have chapters you've overlooked, and you'll need to add to your book too.

III. Make a mind-map of each of the chapters for inclusion to determine what subheading will appear in your book.

IV. Research only what you'll be including in your book, and nothing more. This will save you hours of unnecessary research and ensure you stay on schedule and complete your book in a flash. If you become inspired to research something else, remember it, and save it for another book project.

CHAPTER 5

HOW TO WRITE HYPNOTIC CHAPTERS THAT BOTH FASCINATE AND INFORM YOUR NICHE AND MAKE THEM WANT TO READ MORE AND MORE

A book can have great content; however, if the reader's not engaged, entertained, and loving what you're teaching and how you're teaching it to them, they'll more than likely disengage and stop reading. Imagine reading a book that is more boring than what's going on around you in your everyday life. Would you want to keep reading that book or get out there and do some living? Most readers want to learn what they 'want' to learn. As an educator and writer it's your job to make them want to learn. For this reason, I've decided to share with you my exact system for writing chapters.

If you follow this astonishingly simple; yet, powerfully effective outlining system, you will not only hypnotically captivate your reader's attention and educate them on your topic, you'll also magnify the chances that you gain instant credibility, likeability, and likely become the go-to celebrity authority in your niche. I mean, imagine your book being the industry 'bible' for your niche. How amazing would that be, and how many more copies of your book would you likely sell—not to mention ensure you create so much goodwill within your niche that any future books you write will be well received.

I mean look at Stephen King. He's accomplished writing so many books, and created so much goodwill with his readers, that anytime he writes a new book, regardless of its high-quality (or not) his readership is credit-card ready and waiting to purchase that newest novel.

Now we're not writing a novel today; yet, the same holds true with what we're wanting to accomplish. We're wanting to produce something that's first-class and which contains so much value for our reader that they cannot wait to buy our next book. This is how you build trust—delivering unexpected value.

WHY IS HAVING THE RIGHT SYSTEM IN PLACE THE SUREFIRE WAY TO A SUCCESSFUL WRITING CAREER

When we're going through school we're learning according to someone else's system. We're taught to play by their rules. The reason the system is in place in first place is because it creates standards which can be measured. Your success in school is measured by how successfully you follow the system and comply with what is required of you. This of course (and note they don't typically make this fact known) causes competition. There are the 'smart kids', 'the average kids' and the 'I'm not going to graduate kids'. If you look at this on a statistical curve it would look like a bell-curve. You have so few who will graduate with highest honors, a great majority who will graduate with a general education diploma, and so few who will not graduate at all.

Systems are present in the workplace too. Think about a fast-food restaurant. They need systems in place in order to get your food out that drive-thru window as soon as humanely possible. It's how the restaurant owner makes his/her money. They definitely don't want to lose money because you didn't follow the system and play by their rules. No, they'll just replace you with someone who will follow the rules.

So if you don't follow the system in school, chances are you'll land a low paying job where you'll be forced to follow another system you may not (and probably won't) like following either.

The truth of the matter remains, regardless of how you might or might not feel about following systems, they are highly effective when it comes to producing top-notch results with a high degree of consistency.

The system I have developed, and will be sharing with you in this chapter, metaphorically will transform you from a sit-down restaurant (wait 45 minutes to an hour for your food), to the fast-food mecca of the universe; where the food is waiting for you on your tray before you've ever handed the cashier your money. And, by the way, the food is finer than the finest restaurant you've ever eaten at. This is a bold claim, but one I'm going to prove to you beginning right now.

WHAT YOU NEED TO KNOW ABOUT THIS SYSTEM BEFORE I SHARE IT WITH YOU

I developed this system for writing how-to non-fiction books designed specifically for the Hypnosis and NLP niche. I developed it so that I could hypnotize my readers with my writing to make the learning curve diminish substantially for them. In this book, I will not get into the fine distinctions of hypnotic writing and communicating, because that's not necessary for you to understand those distinctions in order to use this system, and apply it to your own niche.

What this system does is take a lot of the guess work out of writing a 'how-to' book. The objective of a 'how-to' book is to teach the reader 'how-to' do something. For this reason, a book of this kind, should include some exercises, plenty of subtle repetition of instruction, and some stories and case studies to engage the reader and to show them applications where the knowledge might be useful. Stories by their very nature are hypnotic, meaning they tend to transport the reader from their world into the world of some character and setting. Naturally, we tend to empathize with the main character (protagonist), while we tend to despise the perceptively hateful and evil villain in a story (antagonist). Some stories are less involved and carry less weight and significance when measured up against the scale of how well they tend to transport us from our everyday realities to a journey land. You'll have to, as the writer of your own book, discriminate what types of stories you add to your non-fiction 'how-to' books (assuming you add them).

Because, 'how-to' books are educational I have also researched various learning methodologies and frameworks and found one that I believe works the best. It is a framework that was developed by Dr. Bernice McCarthy. What I love about this framework is that it covers the different learning styles that people have, and allows you to present information in a way that effectively covers all the bases. This framework is known as the 4MAT framework.

The 4MAT framework is composed of four quadrants: (a) Why, (b) What, (c) How, and (d) What if. Each quadrant is split in two representing a left brain/right brain connection. Left brain thinkers are linear, systematic, logical, and critical in their thinking. People who are dominantly right brain are creative, conceptual, and more abstract in their thinking and doing processing. When you teach using this 4MAT system you ideally are flipping back and forth between left brain and right brain instruction, as you move from quadrant 1 all the way around to quadrant 4. Sequentially, in this order, the educator addresses specific key points to involve all four dominant learner types. Here is a diagram I have created, which I use as a cheat sheet in addition to the blueprint I use when I'm constructing my book chapters.

Bernice McCarthy's 4MAT Learning Application Framework

Outer labels (clockwise from top-left): PERFORM, CONNECT, ATTEND, IMAGE, INFORM, PRACTICE, EXTEND, REFINE

Side labels: Where can I apply this information? | What's in it for me? | What are the facts? | How does this work?

CONCRETE EXPERIENTIAL

Quadrant 4: What if? [CREATING]	Quadrant 1: Why? [FINDING MEANING]
This learner takes into consideration the usefulness of something and takes it to a whole new level, wondering and questioning how this might be useful in other contexts.	This learner seeks out meaning by asking why(?)
They learn by trial and error and are welcomes new discoveries. They tend to innovators.	They connect to value and emotions and therefore this is your opportunity as an educator to build rapport with them.
	In this first quadrant you are 'selling' the idea.
In this role, as an educator, you are the 'colleague/equal'. [EXPERIMENTATION]	In this role you are a 'motivator'. [REFLECTIVE]
[ACTIVE] Quadrant 3: How? [EXPERIMENTING]	[OBSERVER] Quadrant 2: What? [FINDING ORDER]
This type of learner learns by testing theories, because they need to konw how things work and operate.	This learner learns by thinking through ideas. They seek facts and research. They want to know what the experts think; so for this reason you must assume the role of a teacher and relayer of facts..
This learner is wanting to know things for the application and usefulness of it.	
This learner wants to be engaged and given tasks and exercises to learn 'hands-on'.	The usefulness of the subject being taught is usually irrelevant to this type of learner because it is more the information they are seeking.
In this role as an educator you are playing 'coach' or 'facilitator'.	

ABSTRACT CONCEPTUAL

Because the graphic has had to be sized down to fit into this book I feel it important to cover it in some detail now with you:

The first quadrant is the 'Why' quadrant. In this section you are going to explain why the topic is important. Your reader, at this stage, is seeking out meaning and wanting to know why it is they should be learning this point you're trying to make. The reader also wants to know what's in it for them learning this material. You're almost taking on the role of a sales professional giving a sales presentation. Another way to look at this is that you're stimulating curiosity and placing yourself in the role of a 'motivator'. I always think about Anthony Robbins up on stage motivating his audience of thousands. This puts me in the right frame of reference.

The next quadrant is 'What' and it involves relaying the facts. You are essentially putting out knowledge and information in front of your reader, like a lecturer. In this role you are the teacher presenting the information the student need to know in order to do the assignment. The application comes later, and at this point in the lesson, they're simply getting a survey of the facts and what the 'experts' think.

In quadrant three, we come to the 'how' which is the application of the information in terms of a sequence. This is the 'process' one takes to put into motion (hand on) what it is they've already conceptualized and made sense of. I like to think of the 'how' section as a series of sequential steps that lead to an outcome. During this phase of instruction you are merely acting as the facilitator and coach. You're not in the game, just coaching the participants to a win.

The last quadrant (quadrant four) is where the student and teacher become colleagues. The student now is discovering how to apply what they've learned to different contexts and learning how it might be even more useful. At this stage the student becomes the innovator and participates in the evolution of knowledge and how it might be applied more intelligently. They are asking questions like: "What if I tried this? Then what would happen?" And, it is through this type of experimentation that new discoveries are uncovered and progress is achieved.

Keep in mind that all learners have aspects of each of these four quadrants in their makeup; however, most often people tend to be more aligned with one or two of the different quadrants.

The rule of thumb I use when I am constructing each of these sections of my book is to construct them in terms of ratios. Here's my general ratio breakdown per quadrant: (a) Quadrant 1 = 35%, (b) Quadrant 2 = 22%, (c) Quadrant 3 = 18%, and (d) Quadrant 4 = 25%. This breakdown accounts for the fact that the: 'Why' quadrant needs time to sell the topic; the 'What' quadrant relays a lot of information to the knowledge seeker; the 'How' quadrant is simply relaying the sequential instructions to complete a task (taking less time); and the 'What if' quadrant is expounding on the potential future implication of the learning, which is something to get excited about, and further reinforces the importance of the topic.

The last thing you need to know is that I use the typical five paragraph essay approach to writing my chapters: (a) I tell them what I'm going to teach them (Introduction), (b) teach them the information using the for 4MAT system incorporated (i.e., 'why', 'what', 'how', and 'what if'), along with utilizing stories and case studies to engage the reader/learner, and (c) I recap the entire chapter in a brief conclusion. Of course, there's more than one paragraph for my introduction, more than three paragraphs for my body, and more than one paragraph for my conclusion. If I adhered to that college essay format I'd have really short chapters that would not address the topic fully. The principle is the same though, just expanded to include a lot more content and thus many more paragraphs and sections. The last thing I do for each chapter is create between 3 – 5 action steps which are actually exercises. This satisfies some of the 'how' category in the 4MAT category; namely, because it gives the reader an opportunity to put into practice some of the skills they've learned studying the chapter. I characteristically, for all my non-fiction 'how-to' books, use a boiler-plate introduction to introduce the 'action steps' section for every single chapter throughout my book. Incidentally, the 'action steps' section is always the final section of each of my chapters.

By creating a generic boiler-plate introduction to the 'action steps' section of each chapter I am saved having to reinvent content, plus it keeps the book more symmetrical and balanced I feel. The reader also comes to expect that each chapter will have some actionable steps to help them put into action the lesson I've just taught them.

If you go back and re-examine the previous chapters in this book you'll notice how each of my sections is methodically structured according to this exact blueprint. One thing I should make mention of is how I often times deviate from the blueprint whereas introducing stories and case studies are concerned. As a tip, stories and case studies can be a great way to introduce a chapter, because they typically introduce a problem, and end with some type of resolution. Stories are captivating, whereas case studies peek a student's/reader's interest and get them primed for learning. When you are selling your logic and reasoning in the 'why' section, it is also a great idea to include some type of story or case that presents a compelling argument for why the learner needs to learn the lesson. Again, this is why this section of my chapter is usually proportioned to about 35% of the 4MAT system.

HOW TO UTILIZE THE BLUEPRINT TO ACHIEVE MASSIVE RESPECT FROM YOUR READERS AND HAVE THEM LOVING YOU

What I've decided to do is present you with this exact blueprint I use whenever I write a book. Some of the content in this blueprint has already been explained in other chapters throughout this book. Some of the content has yet to be explained, though; so please make sure you go through it properly and gain from it what you can.

This blueprint will be your guide as you author your chapters. What you'll do is take your research and elaborate it into an audio recorder; speaking as if you were actually teaching these concepts to a room full of people who had paid you good money to learn what you know about your subject. You are considered an expert by them and thus you should take on this role in your mind as you dictate into your recorder. Also, imagine yourself on stage presenting and you have this room full of people sitting in chairs clustered tight together and it is your job to keep them interested and engaged. The purpose for doing this is to ensure that as you are authoring your content into the recorder that you are not simply stating dry facts; rather, you are making a compelling point about something that deserves someone's utmost attention.

The following is the blueprint I use when authoring my books. It is formatted as an outline, so it will not be as formatted as the rest of this book. This is done to 'markout' the actual outline so you can reference it quickly when you are writing your book.

HYPNOTIC BOOK WRITING BLUEPRINT
(NON-FICTION HOW-TO)

PRE ADVICE NOTES

Come out of the gates strong. Get right to the point.

Introduction: Why the subject is important, and why you've written this book, and why it's a good idea for them to read it. In the introduction you make a promise. In part I will tell you this, in part two I will tell you this, etc.

Preface: Sometimes written by someone else.

Acknowledgements: People who have helped you.

Dedication: This is dedicated to... (Someone you appreciate)

Down Dump: All the bits of pieces and then just write them out. Just points on a subject. New points will jump in your mind. The writing releases creativity. (Better if you hand write this, as there's a connection between your head and hand.)

Write with classical music, or something that you can get behind. Music sooths the mind, makes you more creative, reduces your stress level, and allows you to write for longer hours.

Mind Mapping: Use Nova, or https://bubbl.us/ (free service) to create mind maps, based around the ideas from your down dump.

Then take a Dictaphone, microcassette recorder, digital recorder, or online recording software (Adobe Audition), or Evernote.

Each chapter will be roughly two hours of dictating up to five hours of dictating. Usually three hours is a good estimate for most books. We talk about 200 words per minute, much more than when we are typing.

Note: While dictating use a conversational tone, and talk as if you're talking to someone intelligent and brilliant, whom you could have a good monologue with, as you share your unique ideas.

First edit, go through the whole book and edit it from beginning to end.

Second edit, break up the text with a heading every 2, 3, 4, or 5, paragraphs. Every three paragraphs create a heading out of a point from the three paragraphs.

Third edit, quote for each chapter is added.

End of each chapter, create 3, 5, or 7 things people could do to take action. Always start with an imperative verb, as it helps people to take action. It motivates them to do!

Fourth edit, polish the sentences. Delete extra words, sentences, etc.

Read Strunk & White's **The Elements of Style** and apply the rules to your own manuscript.

Fifth edit, completely re-read the entire book cover to cover and correct the little things you'll pick up. This takes the least amount of time.

50 -100 hours of concentrated effort, assuming you have done your research.

Research will likely take around 200 – 300 hours to find and organize your information. You'll also go through your research highlighting key points that strike you as important and pertinent to be in your book. You'll also be finding case studies and example stories to use in your own book.

Assuming you're writing non-fiction, and on business, for business people, sales professionals, etc., a good source to borrow from is the Harvard Business Review for gaining latest research, etc.

Now, let's get to dictating, using the following template. You'll use this same template for each chapter, and you'll have more than enough content to write your book. The benefit of using this template is that it is an easy formula for providing excessive value to your reader, and it ensures that you communicate well your message. The best benefit, in my opinion, is that it will make the process of writing your book much quicker and less stressful on you, the writer.

Enjoy the process,

Bryan Westra

PART 1. TELL THEM WHAT YOU'RE GOING TO TELL THEM

Topical List:

- I. Topic/Question/Chapter
- II. Topic/Question/Chapter
- III. Topic/Question/Chapter
- IV. Topic/Question/Chapter
- V. Topic/Question/Chapter
- VI. Topic/Question/Chapter
- VII. Topic/Question/Chapter
- VIII. Topic/Question/Chapter
- IX. Topic/Question/Chapter
- X. Topic/Question/Chapter

PART 2. TELL THEM MORE IN DEPTH ABOUT EACH TOPIC FROM LIST ABOVE (one by one)

I. Explain Topic I.
    a. Why do you need to learn this
        i. Hypnotic Story

a. Start with an EVENT or ROUTINE
b. EVENT or ROUTINE is INTERRUPTED in some way
c. Someone has to be CHANGED, emotionally affected through the experience (Emotional/Hypnotic Theme, i.e. anger, fear, love, happiness).
d. REPURPOSE an earlier EVENT or ROUTINE (This is certainly optional, but reincorporation is an elegant way of coming full circle so you can tell eloquent stories.)

2. Nested Loop Pattern

a. Start telling a story, near climax (usually 1/3 through your story), break it off using a hard or soft break (hard is an abrupt end and begin another completely different story/soft is subtle fade into the next story from the one you have been telling), begin another story; repeat, 5 – 12 stories, then after last story, finish it, and then in reverse order start completing the stories preceding each story above it.) Note: Interruption creates amnesia, like when being interrupted by a waiter in a restaurant. It also creates importance and intrigue in the mind of the listener. In fact, people's minds will search for a resolution over and over again, for as long as it takes (years even), until their minds are satisfied. Note 2: Hard breaks create greater amnesia and greater effect, however, soft breaks are less noticeable.

b. Incorporate hypnotic themes (relaxation, comfort, fear, love, happiness, etc.).

c. Incorporate emotionally laden language, as emotions or states induce behavior/action (e.g., excitement is a buying state).
d. Incorporate hypnotic language patterns.
e. Use variations of different types of stories (e.g., metaphors, fables, etc.).
f. Incorporate extended quotes (e.g., My friend Douglas, told me, "To the extent you understand hypnosis, you understand how possible it is to hypnotize others, merely using these hypnotic stories.").

       g. Embedded Commands (Analogue Marking)
       h. Artfully vague ambiguous language (e.g., be aware/beware).
       i. Sensory (Visual, Auditory, Kinesthetic, Olfactory, and Gustatory)
       j. Awareness Predicates (Notice, Discover, Be Aware, Remember, Imagine, Pretend, etc.)
       k. Syntax (e.g., enunciating a particular word, or rearranging a sentence to create a different effect, emotions, feeling, response, etc.)
3. Hypnotic Hero's Journey (Monomyth)
       a. Character begins in normality; that

is to say, a normal, relatable, environment. Note: this is important because this creates a contrast between new world/environment he/she will be entering.

b. Character undergoes an initiation (e.g., invited into a whole new world/environment). Note: The character resists change and initially refuses the initiation.

c. Character gets a mentor (e.g., wise guide, etc.)

d. First Threshold (e.g., crossing over into the new world)

e. Coming to terms with the new

world (e.g., character accepts change/metamorphosis).
f. Trials (e.g., trials, tests, ordeals, etc.) that create transformation. Usually this stage is where some failure happens and these trials usually happen in groups of three.
g. Love/God Experience (e.g., significance of higher consciousness/meaning). This is where the listener's state is emotionally induced and impacted greatly.
h. Material Temptations that lead to abandonment of the journey or quest.

i. Atonement (e.g., with power possessing character, usually a father figure).
j. Apostasis (e.g., someone dies physical or death to their self to live in divine knowledge, love, compassion, bliss, etc.)
k. Ultimate Boon (e.g., when the character achieves mission)
l. No Return (e.g., character doesn't want to return to normality).
m. Flight (e.g., often the character has to escape with the boon).
n. The Great Rescue (e.g., when the character has been

weakened and some guide brings them back to everyday life).
- o. Return Threshold (e.g., reincorporating the experience through integrating those learnings back into everyday life).
- p. Mastery (e.g., character balances between the spiritual and physical worlds) Note: Spiritual may be the memory of the journey and lessons learned of a higher nature; used to help him/her in the return to life as it was, but changed, majorly.

ii. Success Story

1. Problem (e.g., I lost my wallet!)
    a. Search for solution (e.g., I turned my house upside-down, trying to find it.)
    b. Us v. them (Someone finding fault or looking down on the main character, i.e., you) (e.g., my father called me stupid, and would never amount to anything, ever, period!)
    c. Find solution (e.g., Out of the blue I received a phone call from an honest man, telling me, "I found your wallet at the bar, cleaning up last night.")

                d. Surprise or shock (I couldn't believe I had that drunk, that I left it there!)
                e. Problem solved/great resolve (e.g., I took that experience and invented a wallet GPS tracking chip, and now I'm a millionaire!)
            iii. Case Study
                1. Google Scholar Search
                2. Books at library (or: personal library)
        b. What is the theory behind it?
        c. How do I do it?
        d. What if I did it what might happen? What if I didn't what might then?

(NOTE: REPEAT THIS PROCESS WITH ALL THE TOPICS IN PART 1's LIST)

PART 3: TELL THEN WHAT YOU JUST TOLD THEM

(QIUCK SUMMARY OF ALL TOPICS AND LIST OF IMPORTANT POINTS)

1. Summary:
    a. Recap Points
        i. Point 1.
        ii. Point 2.
        iii. Point 3.
        iv. Point 4.
        v. Point 5.
        vi. Point 6.
        vii. Point 7.
        viii. Point 8.
        ix. Point 9.
        x. Point 10.

PART 4: INSTANT ACTION STEPS

1. This last section makes the chapter actionable. It takes the knowing, and turns it into applied doing.

a. Give an explanation of why this is important based off Pfeffer and Sutton's, *The Knowing-Doing Gap* (2000).

   i. Topic 1:(Exercise)
   ii. Topic 2: (Exercise)
   iii. Topic 3: (Exercise)
   iv. Topic 4: (Exercise)
   v. Topic 5: (Exercise)
   vi. Topic 6: (Exercise)
   vii. Topic 7: (Exercise)
   viii. Topic 8: (Exercise)
   ix. Topic 9: (Exercise)
   x. Topic 10: (Exercise)

PART 5: PASSAGE BOXES

I. This is where you go back and use quote boxes and relevant relative passages that could help your particular topic out.

WHAT IF YOU REPURPOSE THIS BLUEPRINT

One of the things like about this blueprint is that it is not only systematic whereas writing books is concerned; yet, rather, it's a great outline for delivering content in other formats as well.

When I decided to write this book I decided to also create a training course around the book to create another stream of passive income from, but also to help those students and readers who really wanted a richer understanding of everything in this book.

So I've actually been authoring an online video course as well. In creating the videos for the course offering I found myself straightaway using the blueprint to teach this material on the video as well. It has worked out perfectly.

Some advice though: Don't be discouraged by this long drawn out blueprint. It only looks complex, but it really isn't. Once you have constructed a chapter or two using the blueprint, chances are you'll only return to it at the beginning of each new chapter and only to get your bearings. I would hazard a guess that by the time you get to the last couple chapters of your book you'll not even need the blueprint, and that it will have become imprinted in your mind permanently.

What's especially nice about learning the 4MAT system, and remembering in sequence Why, What, How, and What if, is that you can expound on nearly any topic, on the spot, if you're ever put on the spot and asked to give a speech or lecture. You'll introduce the topic, explain why it's important, give the facts and what your audience needs to know about the topic, transition into how they can apply the information usefully, and suggest ideas about where in the future they may be able to repurpose it for other purposes. Then you'll recap, propose a next course of action, and graciously accept your applause. Taking this a step further, you could also share a metaphor or a story that sets the stage during your introduction or when you're making an argument trying to persuade your audience to believe your persuasions about your topic. You could also incorporate a case study to make yourself sound intelligent and well read; that is, of course, putting it in your own words as you paraphrase the parts of the case you recall. The more you are able to spice up the content and make it interesting the more well-received you will be by your reader, viewer, audience, or even workshop participants for that matter.

This leads into other ways that you might, on your own, be able to think about ways of utilizing this system I've created for delivering content. Maybe you'll want to add some embellishments I've yet to come up with on my own. Perhaps you'll discover other context it can be used in also. It could be that you'll keep this memorized so that whenever you have a conversation with someone and your knowledge of a subject is called into question, you can emphatically deliver the content using this blueprint and be well-received and approved of by your doubters.

RECAP

In this chapter we covered a lot of ground. We started with an introduction to the book writing blueprint that I have developed and refined for writing non-fiction 'how-to' books to where they will be well received by your audience. I expressed to you the importance of having a dynamite system that consistently gets results. You do not want to rely on merely adding in random content and calling it a book. Believe it or not, it actually takes a lot more time being random, than it does utilizing my methodical well-organized blueprint. Time is of the essence too if you want to write a book in a flash. Second guessing what goes where and then having to make changes later will not get you very far, and you'll be much more likely to quite altogether and never return to writing your book.

The next thing we investigated was the 4MAT system and how it fits into the blueprint. This system allows you to teach content from an educator's perspective. By following the guidelines of the blueprint you are walked step-by-step through each sequence, making writing your book cookie-cutter simple. The genius of the 4MAT system is it covers not only left-right brain learning styles, but also it covers the four learning preferences of learners. By assimilating this 4MAT system into the book writing blueprint it encourages you to become a better instructor and a better writer.

Finally, the blueprint was delivered to you in whole, exactly as I have it set before me when I'm writing a book. It contains my news and miscellaneous writing resources, while also reviewing some of the content you've already learned, as well as touches on some of what's to come down the road in the book.

The blueprint, I told you, will take only a little time to learn. Possibly only a couple chapters will it take for you to construct future chapters without having to use it. One thing you can be assured of is that it will be learnt and you will understand the entire blueprint clearly, and understand how to construct future chapters in your book with immense ease. What you will likely run into if you're not careful is long chapters. You have to be careful of this as you could end up with a 200+ page book and only have 3 – 5 chapters covered. The blueprint makes it so you never have to think about what to write, and can keep on writing without any real effort. It really is a great resources that will let you write first-class books without effort and all within a single day—if you wish.

ACTION STEPS

Let me suggest that to the extent you do these exercises will be the extent you are successful in completing this program. By 'program' I mean that you'll finish your book today, or really soon (a flash), and not sometime else, or possibly never.

You want to succeed don't you? By that, I mean you want to get this book written now and out to market as soon as possible so you gain the benefits you're desiring from writing this book. Let me answer that for you: The answer is and emphatic: "Yes! I want to get my book written in a flash so I can enjoy the benefits of having a first-class book published and making me money well into the future which readers will love me for writing and gain tons of value from!"

Good! Do these exercises real quick and let's 'hop' to it, shall we? After all, we've got a book to get written!

II. Take a few minutes to understand the 4MAT system, as this is an essential ingredient that is assimilated into the Hypnotic Book Writing Blueprint. Practice explaining in the 4MAT method, an easy generic subject you have some common-sense knowledge about.

III. Make a copy of the blueprint to have in front of you as a cheat sheet to help you write your book faster. Take notes on the copy as needed to help you make sense of insights that will likely come to you.

IV. Dictate into your recorder an entire chapter of your book (using the blueprint as your guide). Next go back and transcribe the chapter, cleaning up your sentence constructions properly.

V. Dictate into your recorder the rest of your chapters, adopting this same method. Be quick about it, and never take a break until you've completed an entire section. If you do, you'll likely become confused and have to take time to re-acquaint yourself with what you were in the middle of. This is important. Make sure you take breaks whenever you feel fatigued. Have a bottle water handy as you'll be using your voice to dictate the content. It might help to pace around your home-office as you dictate (alternating between doing research and dictating).

CHAPTER 6

THE HOLISTIC ORGANIZATION PRINCIPLE TO HELP YOU SUCCEED

When I was in sales, selling yellow pages advertising I learned very quickly that my income depended on how organized I was. The more organized I was, the more money I earned. There have been a lot of great books on time management written. I like those books, as they happen to be small and succinct and they give you exactly what you need to get organized, manage your time, and achieve your goals in a timely fashion.

This chapter is designed to teach you how to get organized with your writing, stay focused, and complete your writing objectives in a straightforward timely manner. Just like I explained in the last chapter how systems are the key to producing predictable output levels, well, a critical aspect of any great system is managing it efficiently by being organized and prepared to make the best use of your time.

It may not seem like it right at the moment, because you've probably only *mentally* been writing your book in your mind up to now. The last exercise I had you do was a test to determine how determined you are to get started. Remember what I said in the introduction; openly: it is critical that you finish this entire book one time through, and then that you understand that each chapter, though some of the content repeats, does not necessarily fit in any particular order. Had you not known how to do research and how to write using the dictation and transcription method, it would not make sense for me to teach you how to get organized, because you'd not know what I meant, when I tell you that you need to organize your audio dictation files by chapter, and section name, referencing the blueprint, because you'd not have covered that material yet. So for this reason, I have decided to wait until now in the book to give you my prescribed method for getting organized and staying on track.

WHY DO YOU NEED A HOLISTIC ORGANIZATION SYSTEM TO BE ABLE TO WRITE A BOOK IN A FLASH

Shortcuts won't earn you any brownie points with me, because those shortcuts will cause you to extend your writing of your book a lot longer out into the future than had you simply followed the prescribed formula, which I'm laying out for you in this book. Seriously! If you want to do it your way, and you think your way will have your book finished in a flash, then, by all means, be my guess; however, I don't think you paid good money for this book to not want to follow this proven recipe; a recipe that's literally in your hand right now, ready be implemented, now did you? I would hope not.

Why you need a writer's organization system to write a book in a flash is because organization and planning create motivation. And motivation is what you need in order to do something systematically and complete it as quickly as possible. People tend to 'lose sight of this'. They live their lives cluttered, and as a result they lose the habit of putting objects back in their place once they are finished using them. And as a result, their lives become cluttered, and they lose their motivation and their drive to continue achieving solid results. Slothfulness happens.

Organizing your day using a day planner can greatly help keep you on track and motivated. Going step by step throughout the day, planning what you're going to do, and when you are going to do it, has been proven to help people reduce apathy—and get excited and onboard with a project. A step-by-step system is a great means to managing your time, prioritizing goals, and accomplishing what you want to get done. You can also use your day planner to prioritize tasks and create check-off lists.

Lists are very important, because they help you prioritize assignments and rank order them. This means equates to more important tasks getting checked off the list first. If you don't get everything done, at least you've achieved the most pressing items on your agenda. Items of secondary importance can be done at a later time, or pushed back when you have the time to get them done. You don't want to uphold the habit of doing these secondary tasks at the expense of doing more important tasks. If you do, you might not get done what you really want to get done.

Every time you achieve checking something off on your list it becomes a tiny success that can and should be rewarded. This reward can take the form of either a short break or even something else you find motivational. More importantly, those accomplishments will keep you motivated and moving forward, achieving other things that are important to you.

So, when you are writing a book and you want to have it completed, and as 'soon as possible', the goal then should be to first get your house/office in order, and get everything organized. Know what it is you are doing. Have everything, i.e. all your resources, out in front of you. And, when you are completely ready to begin, then start writing your book. Only then at that stage are you in a good position to in fact start achieving your goal of getting the book written. This point can't be underscored enough, because so often when people begin a book project, they'll write 2, 3, 4 chapters and then, due to the clutter in their life, their disorganization mounting, and other things distracting them and becoming more important, they then start to lose interest, and as a result they stop writing, and the book never does gets finished.

This is, in my opinion, one reason why many college students drop out of school their freshman and sophomore years. It's because what they are learning is spread out over a sixteen week interval. Over those sixteen weeks, the student becomes completely 'bored' with the subject matter and dispassionate, and as a result he or she does poorly on final exams and their class assignments leading up to the end of the sixteen weeks.

Time management and organization plays a vital role when writing a book. People say, "I will write so many pages per day." However, if they don't, or if they miss just even a day or two, it's easy for them to talk themselves out of writing their book. It's the same thing as going on a diet and telling yourself you're going to adhere to a certain type of diet, and then the minute you start eating snacks or junk food or something out of the blue that is offered to you, possibly you offering it to yourself as a reward for your good dieting behavior, you instantly fall off the horse and don't get back on. Well, it's the same exact thing that happens when someone wants to write a book. You want to get your messages down as soon as possible. You want to stay motivated. And, you want to crank it out and get it finished and through with, because you only have a small window of opportunity in which you'll stay fully engaged with your writing, and actually do it. The longer you go without typing, the more likely it is you'll never finish your book. For this good sense, I recommend going full throttle and working as quickly as possible to get your first draft finished. Once you have that first draft done, you start feeling a little excited, and start believing you'll actually get the book written sometime really soon. This is very motivational. It helps you complete your book, and do a fine job.

WHAT YOU NEED TO KNOW ABOUT ORGANIZATION AND TIME MANAGEMENT

So, what do you need to know as far as organization goes? Organization requires that you have a system setup specifically for your writing project. This means 'having the right programs' and, it means having everything organized at your work station. It also means having your cell phone off when it's time to write. It also means knowing what you need to have in front of you at your disposal in order to be able to make this thing 'happen' so that you can get this book rolled out in a flash.

You also want to be in a 'distraction free' zone. If you're not, you'll likely become fatigued and stressed and unable to concentrate at all on your writing. When you're sitting down for several hours, it's easy to get uncomfortable and cantankerous. Know yourself well enough to know when it's time to get up and then take a break.

When you do take a break, make sure to complete whatever section it is you are working on first, before you take that break. If you don't, you stand a chance of coming back to your work station, not knowing where you left off, and then having to take the additional time to go back and try and figure it all out. This can cause even more stress. If you will, finish the section you are currently working on first, before you take your break, then; when you get back to your workstation, you'll find that you are ready to get started working on something fresh as you move on to that next new section. It makes the writing process flow so much smoother. You'll be glad you took this advice.

HOW TO GET ORGANIZED TO WRITE YOUR BOOK IN A WAY THAT WORKS FOR YOU

So, how do you actually get organized? What is really the key to being organized and staying that way when you are writing? The key is to first get rid of all the things at your work station that are not necessary. This means getting rid of old water bottles that might be sitting on your desk. It means getting rid of old sticky notes, i.e., post-it notes that just happen to be tacked up anywhere and everywhere, willy-nilly. It also means organizing your tack board (if you have one). Tack boards are useful to writers as you may want to write down ideas and have them in front of you to remember as key points later. You want to make sure everything is clean and organized—distraction free. You want to make sure that your phone is off. You want to make sure that you have plenty of lighting for when the sun goes down.

One thing that happens to me, or used to, is that I'd be writing during daylight hours and relying on the sun to light my office. I'd become so focused on my writing, that I was unaware when it became so dark that it was actually affecting my writing capacity. You want to make sure you can see your keys and that you have plenty of light. You shouldn't read when it's dark, because it's hard on your eyes. Basically, you want to make sure that everything you need is right there beside you, because the more you have to get up and leave your workstation the less writing gets done. So make sure everything is right there within reach.

The other thing I advise is that you have some way to write down a daily schedule each morning. You can use either a software program, or a day planner for the purpose of marking out 'certain aspects of your book' that need to be completed within a certain time throughout the day. It could be that you do this every thirty minutes or it could be that you have longer sections of your book completed over longer periods, but, by writing down your to-do list, and having it out in front of you, something about doing this psychologically and physiologically keeps you working faster. It is like a runner knowing that a stopwatch has been clicked, and that they are being timed—they run faster and harder. Knowing you have a certain time in which something has to be done, is very motivational and will help you write more, and rapidly.

HOW TO WRITE A FIRST CLASS BOOK IN A FLASH • 167

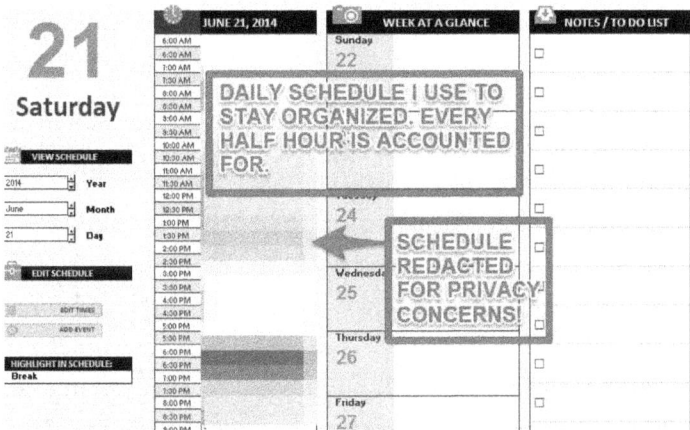

DAILY SCHEDULE I USE TO STAY ORGANIZED. EVERY HALF HOUR IS ACCOUNTED FOR.

SCHEDULE REDACTED FOR PRIVACY CONCERNS!

This is motivational. It is motivational, because you have a desired outcome that's staring you in the face. And you know that the benefits of achieving that outcome are a reward that is simply 'priceless', because you've already decided that this is what you want and there are certain benefits to getting what you want. And whatever those benefits happen to be for you it is entirely okay. Whatever motivates you, whatever keeps you from being frustrated, however you can manage your time wisely, these factors are going to be what you need to implement into your Holistic Organization System.

WHAT IF YOU ORGANIZE HOLISTICALLY AND FIND YOURSELF EXPERIENCING TERRIFIC RESULTS INSTANTANEOUSLY

So, what if we implement all of the things I suggest—for example, having a day planner that you can go through each day, marking off certain events that you need to get done by a certain time so that you then have some type of a direction, i.e. a focus; that is to say, something that can motivate you and keep you grounded, and then, at the same time, allow for some flexibility, in case you need to take a break or you need to run an errand, etc. But still allowing for that regular room to be there so that by the end of the day, you know you've accomplished your goal, and you've gotten what you wanted to get done and completed.

What if you have a cell phone, and on that cell phone, you have a certain application that could help you with time management? Maybe you have an appointment setting application that will sound whenever you need to have something done? It could even be a stop watch application that is all the time ticking down. Now, one thing you want to be careful of is you want to be careful that if you are looking at the clock all the time, and you are focused on the countdown, it is probably going to prevent you from focusing on what's in front of you—namely your book. So, for that matter, it might be a good idea not to rely so heavily on the clock in front of you. Just keeping yourself on par with a mental time frame in terms of how long you have before you need to start your next task might be more appropriate. And if you can succeed in beating that goal, that would be more incentive for you, which will encourage you to work even harder and attain even more by the end of the day. And how remarkable will that feel when you get to the end of the day and your entire book is finished.

If you organize your time and workspace holistically you'll see better results—that's for sure.

RECAP

In this chapter we looked at a holistic system for working more efficiently as you write your book. Every writer has their own process. By holistically managing what's going on around you in your environment, you stand to gain more in the way of writing.

Tiny rewards are motivation for us writers. When you're typing away at a keyboard for an hour, and you've just finished a long section, you can and should reward yourself with a break. It has been proven that taking breaks regularly actually helps accomplish getting more done, because the brain has time to process everything.

Each time you go back to writing, you're starting on a brand new section of your book. This means something new and something different, which in my experience equals something desirable and exciting to begin working on. Then once you finish that section, you're ready for another break.

I also stressed to you the importance of interferences and what to do about them. Smartphones may offer many useful apps for managing and prioritizing your schedule and to-do lists; however, when your phone is on it probably means someone will be calling you and you'll more than likely take the call—a major cause for not getting much done.

When I write I block out all interferences. I write during a time of the day when I won't be disturbed by anybody. I know I have a tiny window of time to get a lot done, so I don't procrastinate or waste that time. Instead, I take advantage of it and I always end up getting a lot more done than I thought I would.

I didn't mention it earlier, but bestselling author Brian Tracy, listens to classical music when he writes. He says it calms him down and lets him get more done.

Writing is a mental exertion that can wear you out just as fast as or faster than physical exertion. When you're writing you're also mentally engaged, constantly in your head. Your brain needs time to decompress. Classical music has been proven through scientific research to help people work longer without as much mental fatigue. Many writers swear by it, and it may be a strategy you want to exercise into your process.

ACTION STEPS

Let me suggest that to the extent you do these exercises will be the extent you are successful in completing this program. By 'program' I mean that you'll finish your book today, or really soon (a flash), and not sometime else, or possibly never.

You want to succeed don't you? By that, I mean you want to get this book written now and out to market as soon as possible so you gain the benefits you're desiring from writing this book. Let me answer that for you: The answer is and emphatic: "Yes! I want to get my book written in a flash so I can enjoy the benefits of having a first-class book published and making me money well into the future which readers will love me for writing and gain tons of value from!"

Good! Do these exercises real quick and let's 'hop' to it, shall we? After all, we've got a book to get written!

I. Clear your workspace and organize everything that's a possible distraction for you.

II. Develop a time management system that works for you. It could be a day planner, a smartphone application, a notebook where you can prioritize and make to-do lists. Whatever it happens to be just make sure you have a method for prioritizing everything writing related.

III. Make a flexible writing schedule that gives you plenty of breaks and time to 'step away' from your writing from time to time. It is important to keep it flexible, yet prioritized, because life happens and being too rigid will cause you to lose your motivation.

IV. Keep to a schedule and begin writing.

CHAPTER 7

HYPNOTIC DICTATION METHOD EXPOSED

We've talked about the blueprint I use to write books. I've shared that with you. We've hinted at doing dictation, and fleshing out your chapters using this approach. We've even looked at ways of getting your dictation transcribed using freelance sites, as well as owning the ExpressScribe software and an Alto or Infinity foot pedal, and doing it yourself. These are all great things to know in order to get your book completed as soon as possible.

In this chapter, however, I want to walk you through my process for dictating and why I think it is a really magnificent approach. The main points I'm going to be covering are: (a) How to dictate/best practices, (b) How to use H1 Zoom, and (c) How to take advantage of the 'chapter' notes in EverNote, which have been organized prior to dictating. First, before we cover all of this, I'll also be sharing with you the benefits of this approach and why I think it is one of the easier and faster approaches out there.

WHY IS THE HYPNOTIC DICTATION METHOD A WINNER FOR MOST PEOPLE WHO WANT TO WRITE A BOOK IN A FLASH

When I wrote my first book it seemed like an eternity. I thought I was doing well when I wrote ten 'book-pages' in a single day. The reality was I didn't know what I know today. Experience really does count for a lot in life. Sometimes the idea of having something finished is motivation enough to keep moving forward. The problem is, people lose their motivations as soon as they discover how much work and how difficult it is to do something.

When I finished my first book I thought mentally to myself, "This will be the last book I ever write." It wasn't though. I actually got hungrier and hungrier and started writing another book, and then another, and another. I've written over a dozen for myself, and an uncountable number as a ghost writer for other people. It is something I enjoy immensely.

As a child I always had this image in my head of Stephen King, living in Castle Rock, Maine, sitting in front of a huge window, in an incredible office setting, that had old world charm, and cranking out books in the most beautiful surroundings. I thought to myself, "This must be an incredible life he has: To be able to write and do what he loves, and not have to punch a time clock, or adapt to somebody else's schedule." I was sort of in awe, and to be honest, I love writing and wanted the same for myself.

After my first book however I didn't see another one coming. The first one had changed my mind about the lifestyle of a writer. It was sometimes hard to pay attention and focus. It was time consuming. It kept me from doing other things I thought were important also. I also had one book completed, and so I figured, "One's enough for anybody—at least I wrote one."

Then something happened. A few months went by, March approached, and I had this thought come to me: "If I were going to write another book; hypothetically speaking, of course, how would I go about writing it so it didn't consume so much of my time?"

It seemed like a random thought at the time. The thought started making me think, however.

Eventually, I found myself online, perusing the different books on Amazon, and I had that thought again. I looked at some of the books out there on 'how to write books' and I purchased some of them. I then went even deeper and bought some training courses, and even attended a workshop on 'how to write books'. I started learning some really cool secrets. I was, actually, baffled to discover that so many people talked their books out using Dragon Naturally Speaking dictation software, and that so many people used voice recorders to dictate their first drafts and then have them sent off to be transcribed.

I got excited. I thought, "Hmm...I could do the same," and I wondered how much faster I could write a second book compared to how long it took me to write the first.

So I did this: I talked my book out. It was an experience that at first I hated. Mainly, this was because I hated hearing myself ramble on aimlessly when I reviewed the audio recording. I then tried the 'talk-and-type' Dragon Dictation method. This was not so bad, however, I found myself constantly having to go back and change words that got interpreted wrongly, and having to think about where a comma goes and how I should word this and that sentence and paragraph hurt my brain a little.

I didn't give up though. I kept experimenting, and that's when I discovered what I call: The Hypnotic Dictation Method. This method takes all the pain and time constraints out of using all those other methods I learned when I was trying to discover new ways of writing a book, faster. I think you'll appreciate this method, because it will have you writing your book like Speedy Gonzales and when you're finished, you'll think: "Wow! I'm finished? That was actually easier than I imagined it would be!" The best part of this method is most people can win with it and get their book written in a flash.

WHAT IS THE HYPNOTIC DICTATION METHOD

I call this the Hypnotic Dictation Method for the simple reason that the experience of writing your book using this method is similar to the experience a person undergoes when they've been hypnotized. They are fully awake and aware of everything; and, yet, not aware. Their time becomes distorted. What might seem like a few minutes has turned into a few hours. It is like they're in one place physically, and another place mentally that's altogether different.

As a hypnotist, I have an appreciation for this type of experience, because I can be doing something I might not enjoy doing, and, yet, be unaware that I'm even doing it, because my mind is focused someplace else.

What the Hypnotic Dictation Method is really, when really considered, is a dictation approach that is highly structured, much like the structure of an assembly line.

On an assembly line the worker comes into work and begins working on one recurring task. After a few hours they might be switched, by the management, to another task. After a few more hours they might be switched to another task. This is done to ensure the monotony of doing the same endless undertaking over and over again doesn't do them in. Importantly, though, the system that makes the assembly line so successful isn't altered; that is to say, the same dull activities are still consistently happening, and production levels are still being carried out successfully.

What the structure consists of is alternating tasks to rid yourself of the monotony and the agitation and frustration that comes with the stress of feeling as if you have to get something done—specifically, something not enjoyable, and even mind-numbing.

HOW TO QUICKLY ACCOMPLISH WRITING YOUR BOOK USING THE HYPNOTIC DICTATION METHOD TO MAKE THE PROCESS SMOOTH AND SEEMLESS

What you'll be doing then is quickly reviewing notes from your research to give you the direction you need to dictate a specific section of your book. You'll then dictate. Then go back to the research for direction on the next section. Then dictate. You'll keep alternating back and forth until you have an entire chapter finished.

However, before moving on to the next chapter, you will personally transcribe one of the audios, i.e. one of the sections, and, as you do, you'll also edit your sentence structure and decide what changes need to be made, until you finish that entire section. Then you'll take a break. Then you'll transcribe another section, again, making the necessary edits, and then you'll take another break. You'll keep repeating this process of transcribing, taking a break, transcribing, and so on, until you have that entire chapter finished.

Once you complete that chapter, you'll return to your research for guidance on the next section for the next chapter, and you'll repeat this entire process.

What you'll have after you are finished with each chapter is a solid, well written, book, that's first class.

The psychology behind this method is in how long you actually spend at the keyboard typing keying away. When you are reviewing your research you're simply looking over what material you'll be including in the next section of your book. It may be that you'll be writing a section of 'why' something is important, or 'what' need to be known before your reader can take some type of useful action, or a section on 'how' they should strategically implement a process to gain some result, or a section on 'what if' they don't take the action or 'what if' they want to use the information in another positive way that's could be useful to them. Maybe it's just an introduction about what you'll be covering, or maybe it will be a 'recap' where you simply restate briefly all the vital points you've covered.

USING EVERNOTE TO START DICTATING

EverNote has some truly outstanding features that one has to admire. I've already shared with you how I organize my EverNote notebook, by creating a separate note for each chapter and labeling it sequentially: Chapter 1 – "Chapter Title", Chapter 2 – "Chapter Title", and so on for all the chapters you want to include in your book. What's fantastic is how EverNote automatically indexes these individual notes and even includes a short summary of the research you have in each note. Here's a screenshot to illustrate this point:

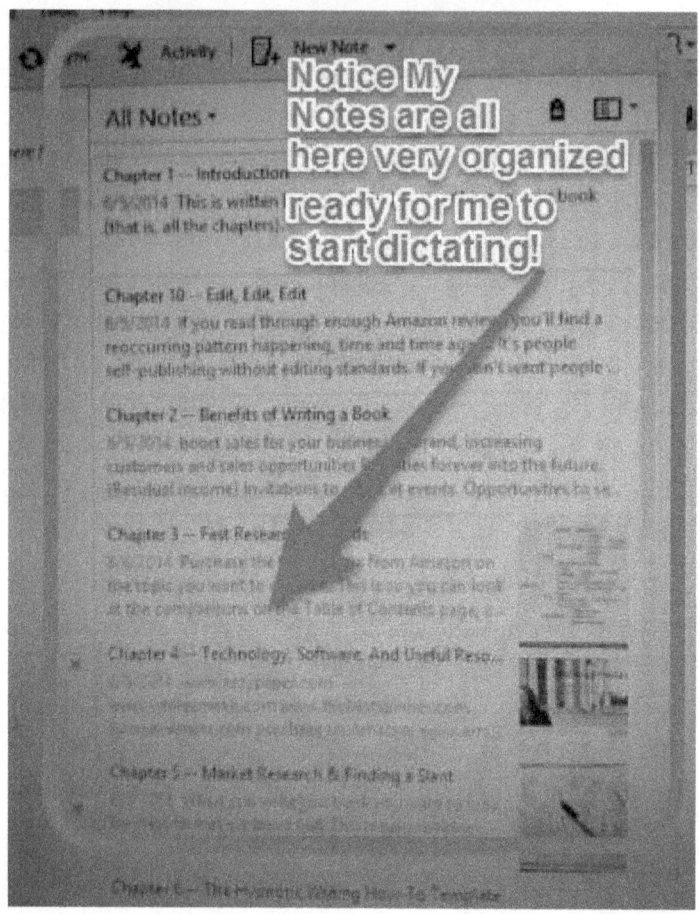

You can simply click on any chapter, and review the research you need in order to dictate that section. As I shared with you before in Chapter 6, I do my best to proportion my 4MAT sections according the following ratios: Why = 35%, What = 22%, How = 18%, and What if = 25%. These fractions represent the quantity of content to be included in each of those sections comparatively. By using this ratio approach I get an approximation of how long I'll need to speak into my H1 Zoom (more on the H1 Zoom in a moment). For example, I estimate that for the 'Why' section I'll speak into my Zoom for about 15 minutes or so. This is a lot of content, when you consider that the average person speaks about 200 words per minute. The 'What' section is usually about 10 minutes. The 'How' section is usually about five or six minutes. The 'What if' section is usually 12 minutes or so.

Even so, writing a section isn't as precise as watching the minutes on your recorder pass by. In other words, it isn't a precise science, and you have to realize that it is going to happen when you'll have a 'Why' section that is much shorter than a 'How' section from time to time. The ratios simply act as a guide to steer you in the right direction when it comes to deciding what and how much you need to research for each section of your book. Don't get too caught up in the ratios. Repeat: Don't get too caught up in the ratios.

EverNote also has an Android and iPhone smartphone application that is free to download from the app store your operating system uses (e.g., Google Play Store). When you down load the EverNote smartphone app, it will sync with your EverNote account. It will also let you record audio files which will show up and become indexed in your EverNote notebook. For this reason you can (instead of running out and purchasing an H1 Zoom, or similar voice recorder) use the EverNote 'record' function to dictate your chapter sections this way. It is an easy free option for many people, and I've used it, and it works well.

USING H1 ZOOM TO START DICTATING

The Zoom H1 Handy Recorder is my preferred method of dictating my chapter sections. The recorder is compatible with most lapel microphones you can purchase on Amazon and other electronics websites.

What I do is attach my lapel microphone to my shirt collar, and run the wire underneath my shirt, and attach the other end to my H1 Zoom. When I'm ready to start dictating my section I simply turn on my Zoom and press the big red button on the front of the device. When I'm finished I hit the button again, and return back to doing my research for the next section.

Why is this my preferred method? I prefer it because the device is easy to use, has manual buttons on it (not touch screen buttons), and because the audio quality is sublime. Most importantly, I like it because I like to stand-up and walk around while I'm dictating. It gets me up out of my desk chair, allowing me to stretch and get some exercise. This is important when you're writing a book in a flash, because you'll be in that chair for far too many hours as it is.

What you need to know about the H1 Zoom is that it uses a Micro SD card up to 32 GB. If you are recording in MP3 format (you can record in WAV or MP3) 32 GB's will give you enough space to record over 100 hours of audio. This is much more than you'll need for any one book. I have written a book using only a 2 GB Micro SD card, and had lots of time left over. You must understand though that depending on the batteries you buy for the H1

Zoom will depend on how long you have to continuously keep recording. The Zoom takes only a single AA battery. Using a Duracell AA battery the Zoom will record for approximately 10 hours straight. If you use a generic battery, I have had them last me only a few hours. There is a battery indicator meter on the front of the Zoom that will alert you when your battery is getting low, and needs to be replaced.

How the Zoom works is simple: You simply slide a slider button on the side of the device until the device shows on. Then on the front of the device is a red round button (the only button on the front of the Zoom). When you are ready to record you press the button and it starts recording. When you are through, you press it again, and it stops.

What's convenient is that the Zoom's default file names are ordered: ZOOM0001, ZOOM0002, ZOOM0003, and so on. This makes it easy to keep up with what section came first, second, third, etc. when you go to start transcribing your audios. You can also, though I rarely do, rename your files once you transfer them to your laptop. Instead, I usually place all the files into a chapter folder, label it, and then add it to the parent directory which is a folder with my book's title on it. I then archive the files online in case I ever need to revisit them for any reason (e.g., a future edition of the book). Here is a picture of how the files actually look when viewed on my laptop:

- ZOOM0001
- ZOOM0002
- ZOOM0003
- ZOOM0004
- ZOOM0005
- ZOOM0006
- ZOOM0007
- ZOOM0008
- ZOOM0009
- ZOOM0010
- ZOOM0011
- ZOOM0012
- ZOOM0013
- ZOOM0014

The nice thing about the Zoom is how it can be repurposed for other book writing tasks. I often do book research by interviewing experts in my niche. These experts I've friended on social media outlets and have a professional relationship with. I can use the H1 Zoom for in-person interviews easily, because the in-built microphone on the device can pick up multiple people talking in a room without having to pass the device around. The device itself is pocket-size so you can carry it with you everywhere you go, as you like. Anytime an insightful thought comes about you can whip out your Zoom and start recording directly into it. I love it.

WHAT IF YOU WANT TO MODIFY THE HYPNOTIC DICTATION METHOD

I don't know if you were thinking how you might apply this method differently to suit your own needs or not; however, it is an easy method to adopt, and even an easier method to modify to make it more useful.

How I came up with this system was simply through trial and error. I would find myself sitting for long bouts of time at my keyboard transcribing hours and hours of longwinded audio files, and it nearly drove me mad. I even to one point where I had hired a couple transcriptionists to do most of the transcribing for me.

I ran into a problem hiring freelancers to do this type of work for me. The problem was the transcriptionists I hired didn't edit the sentences as they went; rather, they just type precisely what's on the audios. So when I received the transcripts back, I had a whole lot of work in front of me editing all that gobbledygook. Literally, I had to go back and reconstruct the whole thing, before I could cut and paste the sections in their proper place in the book. I think, recalling the experience, it took me probably as long editing the document, as it would have taken had I transcribed the document myself and made the changes as I went.

Now, don't get me wrong. I still hire freelance workers to this day. I even hire them to do transcribing for me. I don't, however, send them five hours' worth of audios expecting them to send me back a miracle work of art. That doesn't happen.

You see, people who transcribe, I know this because I transcribe, are pretty good for 15 minutes to 30 minutes and then they tend to get a little sloppy. Accents also make a huge difference in how quality what they send you back will be. If you have a very heavy Australian accent and your transcriber is American, living in the Deep South, you may have a lot of work to do once you get your transcript back. People are only human, after all.

I want to share also that I modify my own Hypnotic Dictation Method too. So I would definitely encourage you to do the same, as it fits you.

For example, with this book, I spent a lot of time dictating and transcribing the first several chapters, and then I hired someone to transcribe a good portion of chapter 7 (15 minutes worth, costing me $5). And I have entirely sat at the keyboard and typed this entire Chapter 8, without dictating anything into my recorder or transcribing anything.

So it really all depends on what approach I want to utilize. Having a sound system in place is important, though you need to give yourself flexibility in how you work. If you find that you're not getting much done typing away, then go back to the system. If you find that you just need a break from dictating and transcribing, then, by all means, sit at the keyboard and type away.

I have already decided that in the next chapter I will be using my Dragon Dictation software to write the chapter. I could change my mind, half-way in, but usually when I start a method, I use it until I get to a stopping point in my writing, and then I may pick back up with another method. My tried and true and most successful method is the one I recommend you adopt also; namely, The Hypnotic Dictation Method. You'll love it, because once you start using it, the book seems to magically get written very quickly, and sooner than you expect it to.

That's when you know you have a good system; when you can use it and have the results you want and then some. So my advice is simply that you take what I'm sharing with you and try it out. See if it works for you (it may not). The litmus test I use to determine if a system works for me or not is by asking myself: "How do I feel when I use this system? Am I distracted? Am I feeling tension in my shoulders? Am I getting fidgety? Do I feel like I need to get up and step away from my computer?" These are all things I ask myself and debate with myself when I take a break to self-reflect.

One of the things I really like to do is to take my dog for a walk and contemplate ideas and let new insights come to me. You may, and I certainly do, get to a point when you're writing when you feel stuck with what to do next. Maybe your process isn't flowing so smoothly and it seems like you're not getting enough done to satisfy you mentally. This can cause stress. It does for me anyway.

So what I do is get up, take a break, grab a bottle water from out of the refrigerator, put the leash on my Australian Cattle Dog, and step out and take her for a walk. Sometimes I take my H1 Zoom with me and when get to a nearby park, I sit at a picnic table and extend out my dog leash so my dog can do some 'safe' exploring. And I start dictating new sections of my book.

I guess what I'm trying to really say is that writing can become addictive. I find myself always writing. I write a regular blog online. I write SEO articles for other website owners (freelance). I write book after book. And, when I'm not writing, I'm usually reading or doing some quiet activity. Most of the time though I am consumed by my writing, or thinking about my writing projects.

Some people say you need a balance in your life and keep a place for varied activities, and not get too into any one functional area, but I heard once, a fellow author (Mark Stevens), while giving an teleconference, say, "I'm unconventional and I do what I love, and my life, all parts of it, are happy for it." And, I've never forgotten this, as I completely empathize with him.

I think technology makes it possible for writers to get a lot done, irrespective of their environments these days. I can be hiking out in Paris Landing, and as long as I have a charge on my smartphone be posting blog articles, complete with pictures of the scenery around me. It's amazing to me how far we've come technologically.

RECAP

We find ourselves at the end of yet another chapter. This chapter discussed in great detail my personal process for dictating and transcribing each chapter I write. We went into some detail about this process and I shared with you the many benefits; most of which include: (a) less fatigue, (b) less stress, (c) much less monotony, and (d) ultimately much more speed and efficiency.

Then I shared with you some of the best practices, and how you could save yourself some potential pitfalls by ensuring that you get away from your keyboard as much as possible when you are setting out on an all day long book writing journey. It may sound counterintuitive, but sitting in a desk chair for extended periods of time and staring with laser focus at your computer monitor, will cause you to be less efficient overall. By taking a few minutes break regularly, you give yourself time to recharge and energize so that you can get back to writing with clarity, purpose, and enthusiasm.

Next, I walked you through the process of how you can dictate audio using EverNote. This method is great if you have a smartphone and don't mind keeping the phone up to your mouth while you dictate into it. It nicely syncs to your computer as well, making it quite convenient.

I shared with you that my personal preference is talking into an H1 Zoom Handy Recorder, because the recorder is pocket-size handy, simple to operate, has terrific audio recording capabilities, is useful if you do in person interviews, and finally, how I like that I can use a lapel microphone to record into, while I keep my Zoom discretely hidden in my pocket.

I also covered with you the note indexing feature that EverNote has, which makes it extremely easy to order your chapters into notes, and add your research materials in a flash. Being able to access what you need on the fly is crucial if you want to write a first-class 'how-to' book in a flash.

Lastly, we covered how important it is not to get bogged down in following method I use precisely all the time. As a writer you need to remain true to yourself, and when you feel the urgency inside you telling you to take a break, grab a water, or just plain quit for a while, then honor that. Writing should be an enjoyable process. Your goals and reasons for wanting to get your book written are your underlying drivers, and let those inspire you only to the extent that you don't trap yourself in a box, and experience the negatives of writing under pressure. Believe it or not, you will get a lot more accomplished quickly if you don't put restrictions on yourself.

Sure set goals, and so what you can to achieve those benchmarks along the way; yet, also don't forget that writing is a creative and enjoyable process that can become addictive. The more you write the better writer you become. For this reason: don't beat yourself up if your first book is crap. Keep writing, because you enjoy it.

The first book I wrote I was extremely proud of. I thought it was really great. Today, 13 books later, I see all the mistakes, and notice all the things I would have done differently. If you were to compare that text up next to my current writings you probably wouldn't even believe that it was the same writer who authored it. It is because my writing has gotten better.

I share this story with you because it is important to realize that the same will happen to you. You will become a better writer the longer you consistently write. However good you think you are now, you'll only continue to get better. This is a very positive way of looking at things, because one thing you know for sure: You're not going to get any worst. Let this inspire you to continue your journey, because it will only inspire you and keep you motivated. As you keep writing your book, doing your best to articulate your points in ways people will understand and comprehend, just remember that no writing is perfect. There comes a time when you just know that it's time to let the manuscript to and time to get the book in print (or published on Kindle).

ACTION STEPS

Let me suggest that to the extent you do these exercises will be the extent you are successful in completing this program. By 'program' I mean that you'll finish your book today, or really soon (a flash), and not sometime else, or possibly never.

You want to succeed don't you? By that, I mean you want to get this book written now and out to market as soon as possible so you gain the benefits you're desiring from writing this book. Let me answer that for you: The answer is and emphatic: "Yes! I want to get my book written in a flash so I can enjoy the benefits of having a first-class book published and making me money well into the future which readers will love me for writing and gain tons of value from!"

Good! Do these exercises real quick and let's 'hop' to it, shall we? After all, we've got a book to get written!

  I. Step into this Hypnotic Dictation Method and try it out. Do some research (using the EverNote organization method I taught you), dictate a section, and keep repeating until you've dictated your entire chapter.

 II. Transcribe a section of your chapter. Then take a short break. Then transcribe another section.

Then take another break. Keep repeating until you have your chapter completely written.

III. Finish your book's manuscript repeating exercises I. and II. above. Get the entire book completely finished, content wise.

IV. Pat yourself on the back. You've earned it. You've completed the task of writing a book. Now it's time to take care of some details, but first: Take a break!

CHAPTER 8

EDIT, EDIT, EDIT OR YOU'LL REGRET IT

In this chapter we talk about editing. Perhaps no part of writing your book is more important than editing it. Most of your time will probably be spent editing your book over writing it. I mean, think about it: You are talking out your chapters, which doesn't take much time, assuming you've done your research and organized it into EverNote.

But, editing, now here's a challenge, because it requires a critical eye, knowing proper grammar rules, and being able to assess your own work objectively, without attachment—not an easy thing to do.

In this chapter I'll be walking you through some strategies that will help ensure your book is well edited, without taking too much time, and without causing you too much grief.

You see a first-class book is one that when you read it you don't struggle to get through it due to bad grammar and sentence constructions. It means, being able to keep your reader engaged and content to keep reading. I remember once when I was in North India, on a long train ride, picking up a John Grisham book at one of the book stalls that was outside one of the train platforms the train had stopped at. I start reading the book, and I couldn't put it down. I finished it just before my destination, and couldn't believe that I had been reading the book for so many hours on end. I loved that book. I was completely engaged and transported into the narrative.

Now we're not writing a novel or anything like that, but a first-class 'how-to' book will have a similar effect on the reader. The reader will instantly know the value, and each chapter the reader reads will be as equally important as the ones preceding it.

Good editing will ensure that your reader is focused on what you're teaching, and not all the obvious mistakes left uncorrected in your manuscript. There is also a perception readers make when they read a book with many typographical and spelling mistakes, which is they start to formulate the belief that the writer is unintelligent. Your content can be golden, but if you're grammar is poor and you have terrible spelling errors your reader will think so much less of you and not care about the quality of the content.

WHY YOU NEED TO KNOW HOW TO EDIT AND WHY YOU NEED TO KNOW THE TIPS I AM GOING TO TEACH YOU

It is easy to want to pawn your manuscript off onto someone else to edit it; especially, because you can hire a freelance editor to do the job for cheap. I have run into a lot of writers who take this approach, and have a lot of success with their books. There is an underlying problem with taking this easy way out approach.

You see, learning how to edit means learning how to write better. When you edit, and you run into an issue with how a sentence is constructed, and you cannot figure out a way to reconstruct it, so you keep on working at it until finally you learn how, you actually become a better writer and able to ensure that the next book you write or letter or blog post that you don't commit the same style error again. Making mistakes is a good thing, because you learn how to correct them so you don't make them again.

Editing can be an overawing task. It forces us to admit that we make mistakes, and many of them. Getting a paragraph to sound fluid and clear is not easy. We think, because we talk our book aloud, that the book will read conversationally in the mind of the reader. It doesn't really work this way though. But then, you probably know this if you've ever gotten a transcript back from a transcriptionist only to be pausing every 10 seconds trying to find out what exactly is being meant.

There are many ways to communicate meaning, but there are some better, clearer, ways than others. Your job as a writer and editor is to find those best ways and make the necessary changes. The more your skills improve more capable of relaying meaning to others you'll become.

It is rather obvious that those who communicate the most effectively are the most persuasive and usually achieve the most out of life. As a how-to writer you are a writer, a teacher, and an editor. To be a great writer you need lots of experience writing. To be a great teacher you need to be able to communicate meaning so others can easily understand your intent. To be a great editor you need to take an interest in the way sentences are constructed, grammar rules, and be critical of everything you read that others write.

As far as the tips I will be relaying to you in this chapter they will help you learn to be a good editor. The problem most new writers have is knowing when their book is 'finished' and ready to be published. As writers we're our own worst critic. Our manuscript is never good enough. We slave over wondering how we might improve it to make it better than it is. The truth is a manuscript can always be improved, but knowing when to call it quits can be quite the challenge to the new writer.

Understanding the tips I'm going to be sharing with you will give you closure on when your book is finished and ready to be sold.

CASE STUDY: QUESTION THE EDITORS TO FIND CLOSURE ON YOUR BOOK SO YOU KNOW WHEN ENOUGH IS ENOUGH

A young writer, at an Editors and Agents panel, took the microphone and addressed her biggest problem as a new writer. She asked the panel of editors: "How do I know when my book is finished being edited?" This is a problem many writers face: not knowing when their book is 'good enough' to go to be published to their publics.

This problem affects many writers. It is nerve-racking and stressful to think that you'll go back and read and re-read your book after it's been published and find an obvious mistake you hadn't caught during the editing process.

We read books all the time and find such silly mistakes that went unnoticed during the editing process. Jennifer, my significant other, is a fabulous editor, and I cannot tell you how many times she's caught mistakes in some of the world's best-sellers. It happens. Is it acceptable? Is it harmful to the sales of the book? Is it embarrassing? These are questions that tend to be answered with the word 'Yes'.

So if this problem affects these best-selling authors does that mean it's more forgivable when new writers make such mistakes? And, how can people know when their book is good enough?

The young writer got her answer finally, after several of the editors on the panel gave a myriad of vague responses. But the answer didn't come from one of the editors on the panel. Instead, another writer in the audience took a microphone and gave an answer that made sense.

He explained to the woman that as you write you edit. You'll write a day's worth, and the next day edit it, and then write some more. Then you'll edit the entire manuscript from beginning to end using your word processor to make more edits. After this edit, you'll print off a complete copy of your manuscript and edit it again from beginning to end, making notes in the margin of things that need to be re-worded and changed. You'll then make those changes on your word processor program. Then you'll make a final edit where you read your aloud your entire book from the first word to the last word and make changes whenever something doesn't sound right, sounds confusing, detracts from the flow what's being discussed, and so on. He said, after explaining these four edits: "That's when your book is finished being edited." The young writer had her answer, and she thanked him. Now she could finish her book.

Learning this four step process can help new writers gain closure and get their book to market faster. When they know when to edit, how to edit, and what steps to take, writers can edit their books quickly and easily and not have to second-guess their manuscripts.

WHAT TIPS YOU NEED TO KNOW TO EDIT YOUR BOOK TO FINAL COMPLETION

Writers all have their own processes for editing. Some systems work better than others. Like what happened in the above case: if you ask a panel of editors how to edit a book, they'll give you more answers than you request. Then it's up to you to decipher who is right, and decide what approach you'll adopt.

Ernest Hemmingway had an interesting method for editing his books. Each morning before he wrote another word on his book he would start with page one and edit his book until he had come to where he left off the day before. Only then would he start writing. The next day he would again start with page one and edit again until he came to where he left off the previous day. He would repeat this editing process each day as he worked on his books. When he had finished writing his books he would go back and edit the entire book from beginning to end.

The first tip you need to know is regardless of what editing method you adopt for your own process make sure it becomes a habit. Hemmingway's manuscripts were clean and well-edited because he formed good editing habits early in his writing career. Imagine, editing your book day after day until it was completely finished. Hemmingway didn't have the spelling and grammar checkers or the amazing editing software that exists today. Good editing habits will ensure that you write better, and that your manuscripts are clear and easy on the eyes of your reader.

The second tip is to invest in WhiteSmoke editing software. I explain how to purchase this software in Chapter 2. This software is the industry standard. It does amazing things for writers. It's one of my best friends. The software is easy to use, and checks and finds things that even the savviest editor will miss.

The third tip is to edit according the advice given in the previous case study. Edit from beginning to end using your word process to make the necessary changes. Then print a copy, and using a red pen critique your style and grammar and take note of any spelling mistakes. When you're finished go back in on your word processor and make all the changes. Then print out another copy and read it aloud to someone and get their input and take notice yourself whenever something doesn't read right, or seems ambiguous. Make sure your friend is completely honest and objective with you. Then go back and make the necessary changes.

The fourth tip is to print out ten copies of your completed manuscript and have ten people read it and edit it for style and grammar. This is a tip I learned from Stephen King.

The fifth tip is to hire a freelance editor to review your final edited draft and have them edit it completely. Because the manuscript will be near perfect as it can be when handed over to the editor they will be extra careful when they edit your book, as they don't want to tell you there's nothing wrong with it and then later have you point out to them all the flaws that readers find and post on Amazon.com.

These five tips should serve you well. You would be surprised how many best-selling authors edit their own manuscripts. For instance, best-selling author Brian Tracy is known for meticulously editing each of his books a minimum of four times. He also reads a copy of his book over the phone to a trusted friend for each of his books. A trusted friend is one who will give you honest feedback about your book, and really help you write the best book possible.

HOW TO PUT THESE TIPS TO USE AND KNOW WHEN YOUR BOOK IS FINALLY FINISHED

The first thing you must do is determine what your editing process will be. Will you adopt the case study process where you edit your manuscript on the computer first, then after making changes, print it, and go to work editing it with a red-pen making notes to yourself about funny worded sentences and the like? Perhaps, you'll take Hemmingway's editing process and make it your own; namely, editing from page one to where you left off each time you return to writing your book?

Whatever you decide, make sure it makes sense to you. Make sure when you're finished editing your manuscript, that you get someone other than yourself to edit it properly. You can find so many incredible editors on some of the freelance sites I told you about earlier. Writers have a tendency to remain too close to their work, losing their objectivity. To guard that this doesn't cause your book to wind up being written poorly, always have someone else review and edit your book. This is imperative.

Next, always read your book aloud (preferably to someone willing to listen to you read it), because this will help you catch many common style mistakes. By reading it aloud you'll be listening to the words just like your reader will be listening to them in their head while reading. Does your book take a 'conversational' and flowing style that is both informative and interesting? If not, you have a problem. A problem correctable by simply making the necessary changes to the sentences and paragraphs.

An important tip I Brian Tracy taught me, which I do with all my books now, is to read, before doing any editing, the book: *The Elements of Style*, by Strunk and White. This is a small book, easy to finish reading in no time, and it will alert you to all the most common stylistic and grammatical mistakes commonly made by writers. This book, if you don't own it yet, is very inexpensive, but, in my opinion, it is a must have book for every writer. Here's a recent screenshot where it's listed on Amazon:

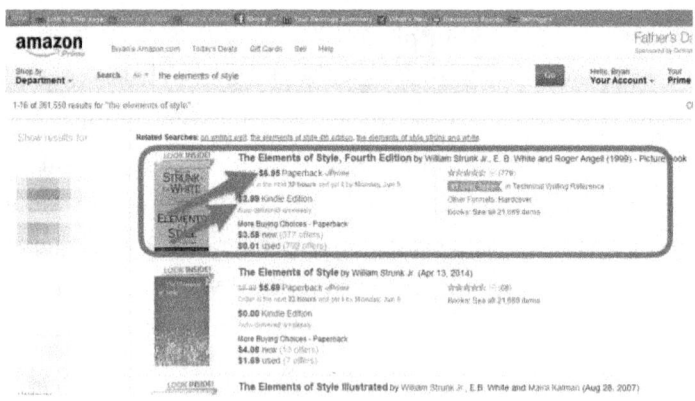

It may be difficult to make the screenshot out, but it's currently listed at $2.99 on Kindle, and $6.95 for the hardcover. Before you edit your book make sure you've gone through the rules in this book. They will not only help you edit your book faster, they will also help you to become a more aware and better writer.

The next step is to use WhiteSmoke to edit your entire book. This is the industry standard in editing software. I owned this software early in my college career and I never got marked off for grammar on my research papers. In fact, I always received compliments on how perfect my grammar was. The truth is, however, grammar is never perfect. There's always rules that aren't broken that should be broken for affect, and rules that are broken that shouldn't be as well. You won't get it right, but you can deliver a manuscript that your reader appreciates. The more you write, as I've mentioned, the more improved your writing skills become. Just keep practicing and learning all the time and you'll become much more proficient at writing. Here is a screenshot of WhiteSmoke in action. In this screenshot, taken from editing this book you're holding in your hands, WhiteSmoke has caught a redundancy issue, and given me suggestions to correct the problem:

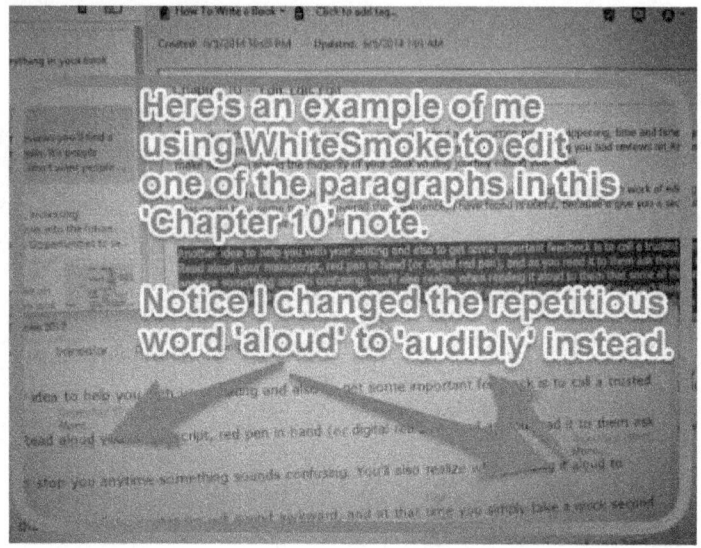

If you cannot afford WhiteSmoke, the second best grammar software, in my opinion, is Grammarly.com. You can purchase a subscription, and it will do a fine job of helping you edit your manuscript as well. I believe you can even try the software out for free, before making a buying decision. I actually use both WhiteSmoke and Grammarly.com when I edit my books. I recommend you do the same if you want to have a remarkably written book.

Lastly, when you've finished editing your manuscript to near perfection, get someone else to read it one time through and have them note anything that doesn't make sense, or anything sentence constructions that are confusing. Then make those changes, and you're finished. You can now publish your book.

WHAT OTHER APPROACH MIGHT YOU TAKE IF TIME IS AN ISSUE FOR YOU

If you're in a hurry to get your book out to market as soon as possible my recommendation is that you do two things: (a) use WhiteSmoke to edit your entire manuscript and make the obvious changes that need to be made, and (b) pay a professional copyeditor to edit your manuscript.

The benefit of using WhiteSmoke is that it could save you some money when you hire a copyeditor, because it will be less work they'll have to do, and the less time they will have to spend editing your work; thus, the less money you'll have to pay them. Editors sometimes charge by the hour. The less work they have to do the less time it takes them. This is why I recommend using WhiteSmoke initially, because it will save you money. What's more, WhiteSmoke is not difficult to use, nor will it take you much time to make the changes. In fact, the software makes the changes for you, you only have to approve them.

A good copyeditor has years of experience editing books. They have made a full-time career out of editing other people's work, and they typically, from my experiences using them, tend to love editing (don't ask me why). They also happen to be extremely efficient and quick. They'll do an amazing job, they usually have their own software, and usually are just as fast or faster at editing as their software.

Good copyeditors will also give you advice based on their years of experience. The consulting advice they give you alone is usually worth the price of hiring them to edit your book. This being said, most good copyeditors are not cheap. You'll have to come off some money if you want to hire someone who is competent enough to catch all the mistakes your readers will likely catch.

Once I hired a copyeditor to edit my Master's thesis, and I was blown away by the skills this person had. They not only edited my paper, they also taught me a good deal about editing and writing I had no clue about. Understand that when you hire someone and they love what they do and you pay them good money and they teach you a lot that there's value coming at you from many different angles. Don't mind spending the money when you know you're getting a lot more value in exchange for the money you spent. It is also a good idea to build a working relationship with a good editor if you plan to write multiple books (remember, writing can be addictive).

All in all, I think if you're in a hurry this will be your best route to ensuring your book gets edited correctly and quickly. Just keep in mind that it will cost you some money.

RECAP

In this chapter we explored several different options for editing your book. I explained to you how different writers have different preferences in how they go about editing their book. Each method is unique, and it's entirely up to you to decide which method works best for you and what it is you're trying to achieve.

I also shared with you a powerful case study that will help you to know when you're finally done editing and can proceed with publishing your book. Next I took you down some useful steps for editing you book; namely: using WhiteSmoke and professional editing software, reading your book aloud to others, having others read your book, and the importance of stepping away from your book, since chances are you've become to personally attached to your masterpiece. You need absolute objectivity when it comes to editing. You'll need to be able to cut needless jargon and sometimes add more to make your ideas more understood.

I also gave you advice from other best-selling authors on how they edit their books. Brian Tracy for example recommends reading The Elements of Style just before editing each new book you're about to edit. This advice cannot be underscored enough.

I explained to you also about the negative repercussions of what happens when new writers get sloppy and don't edit their books properly: (a) reader dismay, (b) fewer book sales, and (c) embarrassment when people close to you and in your niche read your book and cast doubts on your capabilities and authority of the subject matter. You definitely, for these reasons alone, want to make sure your book is properly edited and that you are proud to share and recommend your book with your market.

Finally, I shared how editing should become a writer's best habit. The act of editing should be something you do often and habitually. When you edit, you not only ensure that other people will want to continue reading your book, but also that they'll want to recommend your book to others, but also so that you become a better writer. The more you edit the more consciously aware you become of how you communicate with your reader. You'll learn how to hone your writing style, and how to better teach information to others in a way that they can make sense of.

ACTION STEPS

Let me suggest that to the extent you do these exercises will be the extent you are successful in completing this program. By 'program' I mean that you'll finish your book today, or really soon (a flash), and not sometime else, or possibly never.

You want to succeed don't you? By that, I mean you want to get this book written now and out to market as soon as possible so you gain the benefits you're desiring from writing this book. Let me answer that for you: The answer is and emphatic: "Yes! I want to get my book written in a flash so I can enjoy the benefits of having a first-class book published and making me money well into the future which readers will love me for writing and gain tons of value from!"

Good! Do these exercises real quick and let's 'hop' to it, shall we? After all, we've got a book to get written!

I. Write a customized formula for you you'll proceed with editing. Take whatever approaches you've learned in this chapter and apply what's useful. Everybody has a different nature, and for this reason you need a customized approach that works best for you.

II. Edit your manuscript using WhiteSmoke. Make the necessary changes and get familiarized with the software. Make sure you back up multiple copies of your book, in case you run into any problems or need to go back and revisit previous drafts.

III. Finish your editing and find someone to read your book to. My personal preference is to call a trusted friend and read my book to them over the phone. You'll find a lot of stylistic mistakes and your friend will tell you whenever something comes across as confusing.

CHAPTER 9

HOW TO WRITE A PROPER CASE STUDY TO MAKE YOUR HOW-TO BOOK WELL-EXPRESSED

Writing a case study may seem commonsense to some of you reading this book; yet, to others it may seem challenging and confusing. In this chapter I'll teach you how to write a case study to make your points more understood and to get your reader thinking and intuiting and coming up with new insights.

Case studies are a magnificent way to enhance your book, and they can be nested into your book easily, but also help you come up with more dynamic content to fill up pages. There is a perception in your buyer's mind that equates more pages with more value, and so it helps you to validate in the mind of your reader when you have more pages, that your book is something extra special and that the higher price you charge is justified. Now, be careful that you deliver on the value, and don't just write a bunch of fluff. Readers despise reading a book that's 200+ pages of a book that could have been narrowed-down to 30 pages. You want to deliver value, and for this reason adding case studies to your book is a great method for achieving this.

In top business schools around the world case studies are used to introduce new concepts and problems for the purpose of considering how to solve and react to those problems in the safe environment that is academia. This is to prepare future business leaders to be able to make wise and ethical business decisions when such problems arise. There is value in case studies, because they serve to help the reader critically think and come up with decisions which they might have taken differently to solve the problem being addressed.

Knowing how to write a proper case study is not difficult, yet there is a formula that must be learned. This formula is just as easy to remember as the 4MAT formula discussed earlier (e.g., Why, Why, How, and What if).

WHY DO YOU NEED TO KNOW HOW TO WRITE CASE STUDIES

I've already mentioned some of the benefits of writing case studies, but now I want to take things one step further and expound on why case studies are important from the vantage point of the reader. This is so that you get an inside look first at what the reader experiences so that when I break down for you how to write case studies you'll already have the inner knowledge to make sense of the process.

You see case studies are essentially a story. Stories are captivating and they sell your message to your customer or in this case—your reader. Everybody loves a good story, and we all like to empathize with the situation and the person experiencing a problem, because we all know it very well could have been us, and possibly in the future will be us, having the same problem (or one similar).

So first let me give you a case study and then I'll break it down for you in the next section. For now, just experience the case study as you might were you to read any other case study or news story.

MAKE KNOWLEDGE WORK FOR YOU CASE STUDY

Making knowledge work for you doesn't have to be difficult, and the rewards can be huge. Knowledge is something that can help people prosper their careers, find greater success in the workplace, and even help them to grow their businesses.

Several decades ago two young men were attending their college graduation. They were both 'A' students; graduating Summa Cum Laude (With Highest Honors). Both men had above average intelligence.

Surprisingly, both of these young men went to work for the same firm just weeks after their graduation.

Twenty five years later, both men, still employed at the same firm, were attending their 25 year college reunion, when they ran across each other, and shook each other's hand, and smiled at one another.

Both of the men seemed to be able to communicate as well as ever, and both were glad to see each other.

As they were catching up though, inquiring about each other's success—there was one huge difference that separated them—one of the men was a low-level manager at the firm making enough to barely scrape by on to support his family, while the other was president of the company.

Incidentally, one of the men was a keen reader, while the other was not.

People who tend to read invest in themselves, rather through reading or attending workshops, tend to propel themselves toward success and what it is they want to accomplish moreover than those who don't. By having purchased this book, you're doing something really good for yourself. You're learning how to make something happen. You're learning how to write a first-class 'how-to' book and in a flash.

WHAT YOU NEED TO KNOW TO WRITE A COMPELLING CASE STUDY THAT FASCINATES YOUR READERSHIP

The case study I just presented you with in the last section was actually, one I created from an old Wall Street Journal subscription letter that was written by advertising and ad copy expert Martin Francis Conroy, back in 1975. The sales letter he wrote was so successful it remained in use until as recently as 2003. Over that 28 year period it brought in over a billion dollars' worth of subscriptions. I have paraphrased only parts of the letter, modifying it from the original.

The implication of the case is that knowledge causes people to become more successful. It's reasonable, perhaps, to think this and even to believe it as being true (whether it is or not).

The case leverages the psychological principle: 'fear of missing out' to stimulate readers to buy books and read books. It is a classic soft-sell approach to advertising.

In its original form, it was, as I've mentioned, a sales letter, written for the purpose of attracting subscribers to the Wall Street Journal. If you get a chance, and you want to, read it. It is an amazing piece of ad copy in my opinion.

Now, what makes the case study, a case study? For starters it begins with a title. The title begins with an action verb and describes a benefit. This is common in headlines used in sales letters too. Next there is an introduction, followed by a problem, solution, and benefit.

The case also transitions from general to specific to general. In the beginning of the case study I begin by talking about how knowledge can benefit people in their professions. This is rather general and could relate to anyone's situation. Then I begin telling a very specific example of two men with similar background who experienced two very different results; namely, one man had a low paying job (problem), while the other was in the top position of the company. I infer that the difference was due to one man reading more than the other (solution). Finally, I transition back out to being general again, as I start to relay and suggest that the solution (more reading) causes better results in a person's life in general. Thus reading is a good thing.

Understand that the case study creates certain types of inferences and beliefs in the reader's mind. It is suggestive and causes one to critically think about how they might ensure that they don't end up in a dead end career going no place. It also suggests that formal education alone, how intelligent someone happens to be, nor what someone's background has been, as any bearing on the formula for success in life.

You now begin to see how you can use case studies to sell your reader on your 'why' section of your chapter. Typically, though not always, I will place my case study somewhere nested inside the 'why' section of the 4MAT formula, because I believe it creates a more compelling 'sell' to the reader on why it is they need to learn what I'm teaching. It also gets them in the right mindset for learning the more technical, sometimes dry, boring parts, that's forthcoming—and do so more actively.

What's important about writing a compellingly powerful case study is that it stays imprinted on your reader's memory. You want your reader to remember your points so they can quickly recall the lesson whenever the need arises.

I remember a case study I read in Business School where a girl had started an e-commerce business selling horses entirely over the internet. It addressed how her problem was something to do with people posting pictures of their horses on her site that didn't accurately represent the horses they were selling. The young entrepreneur resolved her problem by creating guidelines for pictures sellers posted, while making it mandatory that they submit more pictures to the prospective buyers when asked. I still remember this case and it was in 2012 when I analyzed it. The point? Case studies help learners to recall solutions other people have had when they find themselves in the same similar situation. Being able to retain this information is useful for the readers of your how-to books, because chances are they'll find themselves in a similar problem situation when trying to implement your books instructions, and instead of having to go back and re-read the book, they'll more likely remember a case study that dealt with the issue they're facing.

HOW DO YOU WRITE A CASE STUDY THAT AFFECTS YOUR READER AND MAKES THEM WANT TO KEEP READING YOUR WORDS

To write a powerful case study you don't have to be the best story teller (though it helps); rather, you only need to remember an easy formula for writing your cases. This formula is what I'll be teaching how to do now.

The first step is the hardest. You have to write a case study that is relevant to the topic you're writing about and teaching your reader. It should serve as a metaphor for the problem people discovering how to do what you're teaching are likely to face and encounter. For example, if you're writing a book on business ethics, the case should be one that relates an ethical dilemma and how it was resolved and how the lesson those involved learned can be learned by the reader too. In this regard we want to find a case study that we can illustrate a problem so our reader can learn by example without actually having to endure the problem. Should the reader ever find themselves in a similar situation, they already have the foresight to know what to do to handle the situation successfully.

The second step is understanding the parts of a case study and making sure yours complies with this formula. The first thing is to use action verbs in your title while also mentioning the solution to the problem which will later be introduced. So you want the title to include the solution. In the one I presented you with above, the solution was 'knowledge', and I've mentioned that in the title of the case, along with the action verb 'make'.

Next you want to introduce the case with some type of introduction. The introduction is usually pretty general, and again discusses the solution in hinting terms. Next, you want to begin to talk about the problem. This is usually done in the form of telling some type of conflict story where someone or some company has a problem that needs solving. This is usually the dimension of your case study that becomes very specific in nature. For this reason you want to be descriptive and zero in on the details. Next, you discuss how the problem was dealt with and successfully resolved (or not so successfully resolved). Finally, you adapt the case to your reader in a very general way elaborating how the solution can benefit them and a wider audience.

So to recap, the formula is simply:

Organize by problem, solution and benefit: First begin by talking about the problem, how it came about, and then transition to talking about the solution and how it came about, finally discuss how the company/individual came to benefit from the chosen solution. Talk in depth about how the problem was resolved.

General to specific to general:

In this I mean talk about how many companies/individuals face this primary problem/need and then talk specifically about one company/individual, then discuss, then reverse this approach in the solution area, i.e. talk about how this individual/company solved their problem very specifically, and then transition to how this same solution can benefit the wider industry or the greater population more generally. Essentially, you're taking an abstract to concrete to abstract approach in which the concrete solution then gets carried into the abstract world of other people's/company's problems, and how it is likely to benefit them.

RECAP

In this chapter we went over the importance of knowing how to write a case study, what its benefits are for the reader and you the writer, and what the secret formula is for relaying a case study in your writings. I also took you through a case study which I created instantly from one of the most successful direct response ad copy letters in history.

Then I broke down this case study for you introducing you to the exact sequence I took to create it; namely: I told you how important it is to use action verbs in your title, and how you want to make certain you include the benefit in the title as well. By having benefit there and making the title actionable mentally for the reader, they tend to get thirsty and want to read more to discover how they too can experience such benefits. Then in the actual case we started by presenting a problem that affects a wide and general audience. We introduced this problem generally, but then we started chunking down into specifics. The next part of the case was a story that detailed a problem along a time line, which ended with some type of solution being found. Finally, we shifted gears back to the wider audience again, chunking back up to generalities, and exposed how the benefits might affect the reader/wider audience.

This magic formula, or sequence, if you will, is an easy way to write case studies in such a way that your reader cannot wait to discover more of what you (the author) has to say. Now they are perceiving value in what you're selling them, in terms of information and knowledge that is, and they're starting to perceive you as an authority and someone who is well-read and expert in your subject matter.

What your reader doesn't know (and doesn't need to know) is that it only took you five minutes to come up with a relevant case study, and another five minutes to write it and make it easy, yet interesting, for them to digest and be able to remember. By creating and including case studies in your first-class 'how-to' books you're making yourself irresistible and unforgettable. This is a surefire way to have your reader sharing your book with other people and returning to your book time and time again as if it's an old wise mentor in which they're completely attached to.

ACTION STEPS

Let me suggest that to the extent you do these exercises will be the extent you are successful in completing this program. By 'program' I mean that you'll finish your book today, or really soon (a flash), and not sometime else, or possibly never.

You want to succeed don't you? By that, I mean you want to get this book written now and out to market as soon as possible so you gain the benefits you're desiring from writing this book. Let me answer that for you: The answer is and emphatic: "Yes! I want to get my book written in a flash so I can enjoy the benefits of having a first-class book published and making me money well into the future which readers will love me for writing and gain tons of value from!"

Good! Do these exercises real quick and let's 'hop' to it, shall we? After all, we've got a book to get written!

I. Write a case study that fits into one of your 'why' sections. Make sure you use action verbs and include the benefit in the title. Make sure you follow the guidelines in this chapter.

II. Share your case study with someone and ask for their feedback. This will help you learn how powerful (or not) your case study is, and what changes (if any) need to be implemented.

III. Let someone read one of the chapters of your book containing a case study and ask them what their favorite part was. Take some notes, and ask some follow-up questions. This will help you perfect this chapter. Do the rest with the rest of your chapters, and get them perfected too.

CHAPTER 10

LOOSE ENDS, ENCOURAGEMENT, AND FINALITY

I'm so incredibly proud of you. You've made it to the end of this book, and if you've been following along with the exercise, you're probably not far from finishing your own book. In this chapter I want to instruct you on cleaning up a few loose ends, getting you some direction as far as getting your book listed on Amazon.com. I also want to present you with some motivationally encouraging words, and bring some closure to this journey of yours (and mine).

First let me start out by revealing that you have all the tools you need now to write a first-class 'how-to' book. I've given you tons of value, because I've imparted all my secrets, and the very strategy I use to write a 'how-to' book. You don't have to go out and buy another book, unless you simply want to. If you're like me, you'll want! I love learning, and being taught other people's methods, tips, and secrets when it comes to things I'm interested in.

Right now I want to take some time to tell you what you can do next to get your book into print form, get a book cover, and get your Kindle book format completed, and all that good stuff.

WHY YOU NEED TO TAKE THE FINAL STEPS TO GETTING YOUR BOOK PUBLISHED AND LISTED ON AMAZON.COM

The obvious answer to this question is because you've put in the hard laborious effort of actually doing what so few people ever seem to get around to; explicitly speaking—I'm talking about writing a book. There is between 200,500 to 1 million books published each and every year. That's a lot of books, about a lot of topics. It may seem as though your book will get immediately buried in the shuffle, and for this reason it's up to you now to start promoting and marketing your book to your target market. Amazon will help you sell your book. Amazon affiliates will even help promote and market your book. However, and of course this depends on your goals for writing your book, you'll more than likely want to take on some promotional activities to help get some exposure to your book, and get some book sales coming in.

You never know if you book might become really popular with your readers to the extent that it moves on to becoming a best seller. I've never written a book expecting it to become a best seller; rather, I write to educate and share knowledge with others in a format that most people respect and gravitate towards. My whole life I've visited bookstores and been fascinated with learning new things from interesting books. What's nice is that most people take kindly to books and even if they don't read, they don't despise reading. Education, which most people get behind, embraces reading and encourages students to read and grow in what they know.

As a 'knowledge-expert' you have an incredibly valuable gift you can share with others less knowledgeable. For this reason you owe it to yourself to get your book listed on Amazon.com, and to share it with the world. Knowledge is power!

> *The hope of democracy depends on the diffusion of knowledge*—Pogue Library Epigraph (Murray State University, Murray, Kentucky, United States of America)

Taking action is usually done up to the last step of the journey for many people. In other words, they work and work and do so much and just before they're about to complete their goal, they lose interest, and give up. I don't know why this happens. I just know a lot of people (myself included) who have underwent this phenomenon. Maybe we're afraid of success. Maybe we only embrace the journey. I don't want you to take tension. I want to see you get your book published and on Amazon.com. It's your purpose for buying this book, after all.

What is it going to take?

How about another case study to motivate you?

Sure!

TAKE ACTION OVER KNOWLEDGE IF YOU WANT TO ACCOMPLISH THE RESULTS YOU DESIRE

Sometimes people get bogged down in the details and wanting to learn as much as they can about a subject that they forget why they want to learn it in the first place. Usually, when someone wants to learn something it is for a particular purpose in mind—for example, buying a book on how to write a book so that they can write a book themselves.

There were these two friends, John and Andrew, both very close to each other—best friends. They liked doing a lot of the same things. If one wanted to go swimming in the lake, you could bet the other did too.

One day, after many months of sitting around, doing little else besides playing video games, Andrew pipes up and suggests that they need to lose weight. Sitting around all day, living a stagnate existence, eating only pizza, drinking soda pops, and chucking down junk food, caused the two friends to become fat.

Well, John agrees.

So the weeks go by and John spends days on end researching how to lose weight, how to exercise, and all these magic potions and pills that are supposed to help him lose weight. Andrew, doesn't do that. Instead he gets to work exercising.

It was weird. John was sitting on his butt, eating a bunch of crap, but Andrew was taking action; he was exercising and pushing back the plate.

About six months go by and the John is still fat, while Andrew is not. Ironically, however, John is preaching to Andrew that he needs to do his exercises in this sequence and that sequence, and only eat these types of foods, and that type of food. John clearly knew a lot about diet and exercise. Andrew didn't know near as much as what John did. Yet, John was the fat one, and Andrew was the one in shape.

We can learn a lot from this case. When it comes to writing you have to write to be a writer. You can read and take in information and learn new techniques, and how to improve your grammar, and all sorts of other insightful and valuable information—yet, to be a writer, you must write. You must take action.

You are at a very critical junction right now. You have just read this book, and you've acquired a lot of knowledge and insight into writing a first-class 'how-to' book. I want to encourage you now to remember why you bought this book. It wasn't to learn how to write a book. It was to write a book. There's a difference.

In order to be successful in anything in life you have to apply what you learn. This means doing something with your knowledge. If you don't, I'm going to suggest that not only did you just waste your money on this book, sadly you're not going to accomplish your goal of writing a book, and this means losing out on the benefits you sough from having a book written.

WHAT CAN YOU DO RIGHT NOW TO ENSURE YOU SUCCEED AND FINISH YOUR BOOK AND GET IT PUBLISHED AND LISTED ON AMAZON

Here's my advice, and what I would do if I were you: I would finish up my book, get it cleaned up and edited. If you like the formatting in this book, you can purchase my template by contacting us through: www.indirectknowledge.com and we'll take care of you.

Next I would go onto Fiverr.com and hire someone to create your book cover. They know what they're doing and will be able to assist you with getting the dimensions for your cover, taking into account the size and bleed. If you're capable of using Photoshop, Corel Draw, Corel Painter, and other types of graphic design software, you can design the cover yourself. If you want us to design you a cover contact us through: indirectknowledge.com. Also, by all means, if you have questions about anything, feel welcome to reach out to us.

Next I would take each chapter of your book and using KDPublishingPro software add them, and get your book uploaded to your account at: http://kdp.amazon.com. This is Amazon's Kindle company. They handle everything Kindle related. This software will help ensure your book is ready to be published on Kindle devices. To set up an account through http://kdp.amazon.com is free and easy to do. Once your account is setup, you've indicated where you want Amazon to send your money (e.g., check/direct deposit), you simply use the software and it takes care of the rest for you. Also, you'll be able to hire someone on Fiverr.com to create you a Kindle e-book cover. Most of the experts on there already know the specifications and will serve as an invaluable resource for you.

If you want to go the 'print' book route you can either self-publish through www.lulu.com or www.createspace.com and each publishing house will have their own account set-up requirements. They will take care of the print copy of your book and getting it listed on Amazon's website and other bookseller sites.

It really is this simple. A lot of writers are only publishing on Kindle these days, because it's easier, less costly and hassle-some, and most people are buying e-books over print books, for many reasons. I personally like the look and feel of a good paperback and so I usually publish in both formats. I can tell you from my experience that I sell mostly e-books/Kindle books.

If you take these steps you'll be in good shape. Remember, you'll be learning a lot as you go through this process. Try not to get upset or stressed out. Writing a book is a process, but when you finally get through, something truly wonderful happens—it's 'set and forget'. In other words, you have your book finished, and now the only thing you have to do is collect your royalty checks and start on your next book.

FINALITY

This isn't the end of your journey, but as your guide this is as far as I can travel with you. The rest is up to you. You have what it takes to write your book. You have the perfect blueprint that walks you step-by-step through the process, and you have all the secrets I can impart to you to make the journey much more enjoyable.

You could have written your book without any book to guide you (I'm honored you picked me as your guide). People have been writing books independently for years, and new writers simply had to go through the motions just like everybody else who has ever written a book.

I compare this book to being a private jet. You see you could travel from California to New York, by moped. It is possible, that you could do this, I'm sure. The ride, though it would be much more scenic, and in the 'ruff' so to speak, would still be possible. On the other hand, you could rent a private jet to take you from California to New York also (assuming you made a lot of money from your book royalties). In this case, you'd be waited on hand-and-foot, served the best champagne, and be there in hours not months. The outcome would be the same (assuming you didn't give up on your moped adventure) but the quality would be vastly different.

This book is a very inexpensive private jet. It's going to help you write your book in a flash, and in a way that's first-class. The quality of your book when you're done, assuming you follow the advice in this book, will be something you'll be proud of and excited to showoff to friends, family members, and anyone for that matter.

Were you to tackle writing the book on your own, without this incredible system I've already laid out for you, you'd likely end up the way I did after writing my first book. You'd be thrilled, happy it was finished, thinking how you never want to write another book, and the book would be one your family, friends, and target-market would raise an eyebrow to and think: "This is the worst book in history!"

Okay, I'm being dramatic, but that is actually what happened to me, and that is why I decided I must write this book to help other people not make the same mistakes I did, or have the same terrible experience. I hope you can appreciate this.

With all of this being said, "I encourage you on your journey!" I'd love to hear about your successes and comments personally. If you want, please email me comments and questions to: bryan@indirectknowledge.com. I'd love to hear from you.

BIBLIOGRAPHY

Hill, B. (2011). *Coach yourself to writing success: Boost motivation, increase creativity and achieve your writing goals: Teach Yourself.* Chicago: McGraw-Hill Co.

Vitale, J. (2007). *Hypnotic writing: How to seduce and persuade customers with only your words.* Hoboken, N.J.: John Wiley & Sons.

Strunk, W., Jr., & White, E.B. (2005). *The elements of style.* New York: Penguin Press.

Watts, N. (2006). *Writing a novel: Teach yourself.* Chicago: McGraw-Hill.

Wood, J. (1951). *How to non-fiction.* New York: Arco Pub. Co.

INDEX

4MAT, 127, 132, 133, 152, 154, 156, 180, 214, 218
academia, 214
academic, 35, 37, 62
address, 2, 1, 106, 120, 132
adult, 6
advantages, 2, 4, 6, 18
alignment, 1, 22
Amazon, viii, 4, 12, 40, 59, 60, 74, 90, 97, 103, 106, 113, 115, 175, 182, 202, 204, 225, 226, 227, 230, 231
Amazon.com, viii, 4, 12, 40, 60, 90, 97, 115, 202, 225, 227
answer, 1, 19, 21, 24, 28, 34, 38, 51, 81, 92, 101, 119, 155, 170, 192, 199, 200, 210, 223, 226
asks, 2
attributes, 2, 3, 4, 67
Attributes, 2
audience, ii, 1, 8, 9, 15, 21, 39, 47, 57, 70, 130, 152, 153, 154, 200, 221, 222
author, 6, 8, 11, 36, 49, 56, 62, 72, 90, 98, 103, 134, 170, 189, 203, 222
authors, viii, 17, 18, 36, 47, 57, 74, 98, 110, 113, 199, 202, 209
benefit, 3, 4, 8, 10, 18, 19, 20, 22, 24, 46, 59, 72, 87, 90, 137, 207, 217, 221, 222, 224
benefits, 1, 2, 3, 6, 7, 8, 9, 10, 17, 18, 19, 20, 21, 22, 24, 43, 49, 51, 92, 119, 155, 167, 170, 174, 189, 192, 210, 214, 222, 223, 229
bestselling, 98, 170
book, i, ii, iii, v, vii, viii, ix, x, 1, 2, 3, 4, 5, 6, 7, 8, 9, 10, 11, 12, 13, 14, 15, 16, 17, 18, 19, 20, 21, 22, 23, 24, 25, 26,

239

27, 29, 30, 31, 34, 35, 37, 38, 39, 40, 42, 43, 45, 46, 47, 48, 49, 50, 51, 52, 55, 56, 57, 58, 59, 60, 61, 63, 65, 66, 68, 69, 70, 72, 73, 75, 83, 85, 86, 87, 88, 89, 90, 91, 92, 95, 97, 99, 100, 102, 103, 104, 105, 106, 107, 108, 109, 110, 111, 112, 113, 114, 115, 116, 117, 118, 119, 120, 121, 123, 124, 126, 127, 128, 130, 131, 132, 133, 134, 135, 136, 137, 152, 153, 154, 155, 156, 160, 161, 162, 163, 164, 166, 168, 169, 170, 171, 173, 174, 175, 176, 178, 179, 181, 182, 183, 184, 185, 186, 187, 188, 189, 190, 191, 192, 193, 195, 196, 197, 198, 199, 200, 201, 202, 203, 204, 205, 206, 207, 208, 209, 210, 211, 213, 216, 219, 220, 223, 224, 225, 226, 227, 228, 229, 230, 231, 232, 233, 251

book cover, 3, 58, 88, 137, 226, 230, 231

budget, 36, 84

buy, vii, 4, 12, 15, 17, 18, 22, 40, 58, 75, 98, 100, 102, 103, 104, 107, 108, 124, 182, 217, 225

case studies, 39, 127, 132, 133, 137, 214, 215, 218, 222, 223

challenging, 7, 12, 213

cheat sheet, 41, 128, 156

clients, 3

coach, 131

Cognitive Dissonance, 103

comments, 4, 36, 98, 115, 233

connecting, 1, 110

connection, 6, 128, 135

consider, 6, 9, 86, 88, 89, 181

consultants, 16

consulting, 16, 208

consumer behavior, 16, 99

contains, 2, 31, 124, 154

contemplation, 6
content, 1, 2, 3, 4, 5, 15, 16, 17, 22, 23, 24, 28, 36, 38, 42, 57, 58, 65, 66, 67, 69, 72, 89, 91, 98, 109, 115, 123, 132, 133, 134, 137, 152, 153, 154, 156, 160, 180, 193, 196, 213
conversation, 2, 33, 153
copy, 2, 21, 22, 37, 64, 104, 106, 107, 111, 156, 200, 202, 203, 216, 217, 222, 231
copyeditors, 208
counseling, 3, 4
degree, 3, 25, 37, 126
delivered, 7, 60, 154
detail, 1, 8, 26, 31, 42, 43, 102, 130, 189
determine, 1, 16, 52, 67, 89, 102, 110, 113, 118, 119, 120, 160, 188, 203
dominant, 128
down-dump, 109, 120
Dragon, 73, 85, 87, 88, 89, 175, 176, 187
drivers, 190
earned, 5, 16, 25, 159, 193

Eazy Paper, 61, 63, 83, 89
edit, 46, 57, 63, 70, 84, 136, 137, 178, 185, 197, 200, 201, 202, 203, 205, 206, 207, 208, 209, 210
editing, 57, 58, 59, 70, 75, 83, 84, 88, 185, 195, 196, 199, 201, 203, 204, 205, 206, 207, 208, 209, 210, 211
educator, 123, 128, 154
elevate, 3, 5, 19, 20, 74, 99
entrepreneur, 219
environmental, 14
Ernest Hemmingway, 201
EverNote, 65, 66, 67, 71, 84, 85, 89, 91, 117, 173, 179, 181, 190, 192, 195
Evernote.com, 30, 52
exercises, 23, 24, 51, 92, 119, 120, 127, 132, 155, 156, 170, 171, 192, 193, 210, 223, 224, 229
expert, 1, 3, 4, 7, 9, 10, 12, 18, 19, 28, 31, 84,

87, 90, 134, 216, 223, 227
expertise, 3, 4, 10, 15, 79, 88, 117
extra money, 4
facilitator, 130
fascinating, 2
feedback, 4, 5, 34, 203, 224
feeling, 3, 4, 20, 28, 45, 143, 164, 177, 188
field, 3, 4, 9, 10, 15, 16, 18, 34, 35, 40, 87, 102
first-class, viii, ix, 60, 90, 113, 119
flash, i, viii, 18, 23, 24, 25, 26, 31, 38, 48, 50, 51, 55, 83, 86, 87, 90, 91, 92, 102, 113, 119, 120, 121, 154, 155, 161, 164, 170, 171, 176, 182, 190, 192, 210, 216, 223, 232
forward, i, 17, 56, 81, 86, 162, 174
foundation, 6
freelance, 58, 75, 77, 84, 88, 90, 92, 93, 173, 185, 188, 197, 202, 203

freelancers, 59, 79, 92, 185
gain, 1, 7, 11, 12, 14, 15, 16, 17, 18, 24, 27, 50, 51, 92, 98, 119, 124, 133, 155, 169, 170, 179, 192, 200, 210, 223
ghostwriting, 59
Google, 35, 38, 66, 117, 119, 149, 181
Google Scholar, 35, 38, 149
grammar, ii, 57, 63, 83, 195, 196, 198, 201, 202, 205, 206, 229
helping, 1, 63, 84, 108, 206
hire, 59, 79, 91, 185, 197, 202, 207, 208, 230, 231
hobby, 2
holistic, 13, 42, 67, 109, 169
How to, 2, ix, 19, 113, 173
HOW TO, 1, 17, 42, 44, 80, 97, 105, 123, 133, 165, 178, 197, 203, 213, 214
idea, ii, iii, 1, 7, 9, 10, 20, 30, 40, 42, 58, 81, 105,

109, 112, 115, 133, 135, 168, 174, 208
identify, 1, 117
identity, 7
important, i, ii, 1, 2, 14, 18, 20, 27, 31, 34, 42, 44, 49, 61, 96, 98, 99, 100, 101, 106, 109, 110, 115, 119, 130, 135, 137, 144, 151, 152, 156, 161, 162, 171, 175, 179, 182, 187, 190, 191, 195, 196, 204, 214, 218, 222
instruction, 1, 3, 86, 127, 128, 130
interested, 2, 3, 11, 17, 49, 96, 105, 106, 134, 226
internet, 34, 76, 219
interview, 31, 32, 34, 70
interviews, 31, 38, 69, 86, 87, 112, 184, 190
intuited, 6
job, vi, 2, 29, 84, 123, 126, 134, 164, 197, 198, 206, 207, 217
KD Publishing Pro, 74
Kindle, 40, 59, 74, 192, 205, 226, 230, 231

know, iii, vi, 1, 5, 7, 9, 10, 11, 12, 17, 19, 21, 26, 27, 28, 30, 31, 40, 41, 42, 47, 50, 52, 55, 81, 83, 85, 88, 90, 96, 97, 98, 99, 100, 101, 102, 103, 104, 106, 107, 109, 115, 116, 119, 130, 132, 134, 152, 160, 164, 167, 168, 170, 173, 174, 182, 185, 186, 187, 191, 196, 197, 199, 200, 201, 208, 209, 215, 220, 223, 226, 227, 229, 230, 231
launch, 99, 100, 102, 118
learnings, 21, 147
legacy, 6
legitimate, 2, 10, 14, 36, 37
libraries, 34, 59, 62, 83
licensing, 3
limitations, 115
lingo, 8
logical problem, 4
loss, 3
manuscript, 59, 63, 74, 136, 192, 193, 196,

197, 198, 200, 202, 203, 205, 206, 207, 211
market, 8, 11, 12, 13, 22, 24, 35, 51, 84, 91, 92, 95, 96, 97, 98, 99, 100, 102, 103, 104, 105, 106, 107, 112, 113, 115, 117, 118, 119, 120, 155, 170, 192, 200, 207, 209, 210, 223, 226, 233
marketing, 11, 12, 13, 16, 21, 22, 32, 76, 96, 226
memorable, 6
message, 7, 14, 56, 137, 215
Microsoft Word, 59, 72
mind mapping, 41, 109
mind-map, 110, 111, 112, 113, 114, 115, 120
mindset, 4, 218
Modeling, 40
money, v, vi, vii, viii, 2, 4, 11, 19, 21, 23, 24, 29, 35, 38, 51, 87, 88, 89, 90, 91, 92, 93, 120, 125, 126, 134, 155, 159, 161, 171, 192, 207, 208, 210, 224, 229, 230, 232

motivate, 17, 19, 24, 168, 227
MP3, 32, 70, 182
natural, 1, 44
need, 1, 4, 6, 8, 9, 10, 22, 23, 29, 32, 35, 36, 37, 38, 42, 50, 58, 59, 68, 70, 85, 89, 90, 99, 100, 101, 102, 103, 104, 109, 115, 117, 120, 125, 130, 132, 138, 152, 159, 160, 161, 164, 166, 167, 168, 178, 179, 180, 181, 182, 183, 187, 188, 189, 190, 198, 200, 201, 207, 209, 211, 218, 219, 221, 223, 224, 225, 228
needs, 1, 4, 23, 73, 91, 102, 113, 131, 133, 152, 170, 183, 185, 220, 229
new writers, 7
NLP, 105, 114, 118, 120, 126, 251
notes, 30, 57, 66, 67, 89, 156, 165, 173, 178, 179, 190, 200, 203, 224
notoriety, 3, 10

obsession, 100, 101
online, ix, 11, 12, 13, 31, 35, 36, 38, 51, 57, 58, 66, 72, 75, 81, 82, 89, 119, 136, 152, 175, 183, 188
passionate, 1, 9, 31, 91, 97
payments, 10
perceived, 3, 10, 12, 62, 114
perceptual positions, 105, 114, 118
persuasions, 15, 153
pitched, 23
practical, 6, 9
problem, ix, 2, 3, 4, 15, 21, 22, 23, 49, 59, 65, 79, 98, 133, 174, 185, 197, 198, 199, 204, 205, 214, 215, 217, 219, 220, 221, 222
procrastinating, 49
products, 16, 17, 32, 34, 71, 88, 89, 96
profession, 2
promise, x, 21, 25, 114, 135
promoting, 13, 17, 226
psychology, 99, 178

published, viii, 24, 49, 51, 91, 92, 120, 155, 171, 192, 198, 199, 210, 224, 226, 227, 230
purchase, 2, 4, 6, 12, 32, 35, 36, 58, 59, 61, 70, 83, 87, 89, 93, 99, 107, 114, 118, 124, 182, 201, 206, 230
purpose, 2, 15, 32, 38, 49, 66, 90, 101, 134, 166, 190, 214, 217, 227, 228
quadrant, 127, 130, 131
quality, 5, 26, 33, 37, 46, 48, 58, 69, 70, 71, 113, 114, 115, 124, 182, 186, 196, 232
quote, 3, 136, 151
read, ii, 5, 8, 20, 27, 36, 40, 50, 59, 62, 75, 97, 98, 104, 105, 108, 111, 113, 118, 135, 137, 153, 166, 195, 196, 197, 198, 199, 200, 202, 204, 206, 209, 211, 215, 216, 217, 218, 222, 223, 224, 227, 229
reader, viii, 1, 2, 3, 4, 7, 18, 19, 20, 21, 22, 23,

24, 27, 28, 39, 43, 46, 47, 59, 65, 67, 74, 79, 98, 103, 108, 111, 123, 124, 127, 130, 132, 133, 137, 153, 179, 196, 197, 201, 204, 205, 209, 210, 213, 214, 215, 216, 218, 219, 221, 222, 223
readership, 26, 39, 50, 84, 107, 113, 118, 119, 124
reading, i, iii, vii, viii, ix, 2, 4, 5, 20, 23, 37, 39, 47, 55, 56, 57, 59, 91, 103, 106, 107, 108, 110, 116, 123, 188, 196, 204, 209, 210, 213, 214, 216, 218, 227
reality, 2, 49, 57, 102, 105, 106, 115, 174
reason, ix, 1, 2, 4, 6, 7, 9, 14, 15, 16, 18, 22, 26, 27, 42, 43, 44, 59, 65, 73, 82, 86, 91, 97, 103, 106, 107, 108, 124, 125, 127, 160, 163, 176, 181, 183, 191, 211, 214, 220, 226, 227
reasons, viii, 6, 9, 10, 19, 75, 101, 190, 209, 231
receive, 4, 21
receptive, 113
recognition, 8, 9, 12, 13, 15, 27
reference, 9, 14, 34, 37, 38, 61, 63, 113, 130, 134
referencing, 110, 160
represent, 6, 56, 180, 219
research, 7, 25, 26, 28, 29, 30, 31, 34, 35, 36, 37, 38, 39, 40, 41, 42, 43, 44, 45, 46, 47, 50, 51, 56, 57, 59, 62, 66, 72, 85, 97, 98, 99, 100, 102, 104, 109, 112, 113, 115, 117, 118, 119, 121, 134, 137, 157, 160, 170, 178, 179, 180, 181, 182, 184, 190, 192, 195, 205
residual, v, x, 10
resources, 3, 15, 26, 35, 36, 37, 50, 62, 73, 89, 93, 154, 155, 162
reviewed, 5, 176
richer, 39, 152
royalties, x, 4, 10, 60, 232

sales, 2, vii, 5, 10, 11, 13, 16, 17, 19, 20, 21, 22, 59, 96, 106, 130, 137, 159, 199, 209, 217, 226
sales letter, 22, 23, 217
scholarly, 35, 39
screenshots, ix, 31, 57, 68, 85
selling, viii, 15, 17, 96, 100, 133, 159, 199, 202, 209, 218, 223
set the stage, 6
share, 1, 5, 12, 13, 27, 28, 36, 37, 42, 47, 48, 55, 65, 73, 75, 95, 99, 101, 106, 108, 119, 124, 136, 153, 186, 191, 209, 227
sharing, 1, 26, 39, 46, 109, 126, 174, 188, 198, 223
Skype, 32, 33
slant, 97, 98, 99, 100, 103, 108, 113, 114, 115, 116, 118, 119, 120
smile, 2
software, 26, 50, 57, 58, 59, 60, 61, 63, 64, 66, 68, 71, 73, 74, 82, 83, 84, 85, 86, 87, 88, 89, 90, 92, 108, 111, 116, 117, 136, 166, 173, 175, 187, 201, 205, 206, 207, 209, 211, 230
solution, 2, 4, 23, 34, 148, 217, 218, 220, 221, 222
solve, 2, 3, 4, 22, 23, 214
solving, 2, 3, 4, 220
Speaking, 16, 87, 175
spin, 19, 57, 84, 111
Stephen King, 124, 174, 202
strategy, 2, 13, 48, 86, 170, 225
stressed, 3, 164, 169, 231
subtopic, 30, 109, 112
subtopics, 30, 42, 43, 109, 112, 113, 114, 117
success, 3, 23, 25, 40, 86, 125, 162, 197, 215, 216, 218, 227
successful, 3, 14, 19, 40, 51, 92, 102, 119, 155, 170, 177, 187, 192, 210, 217, 222, 223, 229
summarizing, 43
table of contents, 40, 52, 56, 59, 110, 112, 120

target, 8, 99, 100, 103, 104, 105, 106, 113, 115, 118, 120, 226, 233
teach yourself, 9
teaching, v, viii, ix, 11, 19, 26, 29, 30, 45, 46, 48, 91, 102, 123, 134, 196, 218, 219
technologies, 55, 57, 82, 86, 93
technology, 26, 28, 50, 55, 58, 60, 82, 85, 92, 189
telephone conferencing, 31
The Best Spinner, 64, 65, 84
trainers, 16
transcription, 59, 68, 75, 84, 85, 160
understand, ii, vi, 1, 2, 6, 7, 8, 9, 12, 18, 21, 22, 29, 42, 86, 97, 106, 107, 119, 126, 142, 155, 156, 160, 182, 191, 198
understood, 6, 209, 213
unintelligent, 196
unquote, 3

value, viii, 4, 5, 6, 7, 9, 11, 15, 16, 20, 21, 22, 23, 24, 26, 28, 41, 48, 51, 70, 79, 84, 92, 100, 101, 104, 108, 110, 111, 113, 115, 120, 124, 137, 155, 171, 192, 196, 208, 210, 213, 214, 223, 224, 225
videos, 16, 32, 33, 36, 38, 59, 70, 81, 82, 83, 84, 85, 86, 152
websites, 5, 12, 13, 36, 82, 88, 182
WhiteSmoke, 63, 83, 201, 205, 206, 207, 209, 211
Wikipedia, 36, 37, 38, 50
write, 2, 9, i, ii, iii, vii, viii, ix, 2, 4, 6, 7, 8, 9, 10, 12, 13, 14, 17, 19, 20, 21, 22, 24, 26, 27, 30, 31, 35, 42, 43, 45, 46, 48, 52, 55, 56, 57, 58, 60, 61, 63, 64, 66, 67, 85, 86, 87, 91, 97, 102, 104, 107, 108, 109, 112, 113, 117, 119, 124, 133, 135, 137, 152, 154, 155, 156,

160, 161, 162, 163, 164, 165, 166, 169, 170, 173, 174, 175, 187, 188, 189, 190, 191, 197, 198, 200, 201, 203, 205, 208, 213, 214, 215, 216, 219, 222, 223, 225, 226, 228, 229, 232, 233

writer, ii, vii, 1, 3, 6, 9, 14, 15, 17, 22, 24, 48, 56, 57, 58, 63, 72, 73, 90, 91, 123, 127, 137, 154, 161, 169, 174, 175, 190, 191, 196, 197, 198, 199, 200, 204, 205, 210, 222, 229

writers, 9, ii, iii, 1, 7, 10, 14, 17, 22, 59, 64, 66, 88, 91, 98, 116, 165, 169, 170, 189, 197, 198, 199, 200, 202, 204, 208, 209, 231, 232

writing, i, ii, iii, vii, viii, ix, x, 1, 3, 6, 7, 8, 9, 10, 11, 13, 14, 15, 17, 18, 20, 21, 22, 24, 26, 27, 28, 30, 31, 38, 40, 43, 44, 45, 46, 47, 48, 49, 50, 51, 55, 56, 57, 60, 61, 64, 65, 66, 67, 71, 83, 84, 85, 87, 89, 90, 91, 92, 93, 95, 97, 105, 109, 113, 117, 119, 124, 126, 127, 132, 134, 135, 137, 151, 153, 154, 155, 159, 160, 162, 163, 164, 165, 166, 169, 170, 171, 174, 175, 176, 179, 181, 182, 184, 187, 188, 189, 191, 192, 193, 195, 196, 198, 201, 203, 205, 208, 210, 214, 218, 219, 223, 226, 229, 232

Writing, ii, 3, 14, 22, 66, 91, 156, 170, 190, 231

writing process, 17, 20, 21, 44, 50, 58, 61, 67, 93, 165

YouTube, 36, 38, 50, 81, 82, 83, 84, 85, 86, 88, 90, 92

Zoom, 69, 70, 83, 87, 89, 173, 181, 182, 183, 184, 188, 190

ABOUT THE AUTHOR

Bryan Westra has authored over a dozen book. He's also the founder of: www.indirectknowledge.com: a publishing house and communications training company. He is also a high in-demand international Hypnosis and NLP trainer's trainer.

www.ingramcontent.com/pod-product-compliance
Lightning Source LLC
Chambersburg PA
CBHW022108150426
43195CB00008B/323